The
MOTOWN
ALBUM

The Sound of Young

Designer: Sheila Levrant de Bretteville

Editor: Marianne Partridge

Consulting Editors for Motown Records: Traci Jordan and Belma Johnson

America

The

MOTOWN
A L B U M

Foreword by Berry Gordy

Introduction by Elvis Mitchell

History by Ben Fong-Torres

Discography by Dave Marsh

Sarah Lazin Books   St. Martin's Press New York 1990

The Motown Album: The Sound of Young America
Copyright © 1990 by Motown Record Co., L.P., and Sarah Lazin Books

For information, address St. Martin's Press, 175 Fifth Avenue, New York, NY 10010.

First Edition

10 9 8 7 6 5 4 3 2 1

Library of Congress Cataloging-in-Publication Data

Fong-Torres, Ben.
          The Motown album / foreword by Berry Gordy; essay by Elvis
     Mitchell; text by Ben Fong-Torres; discography by Dave Marsh.
               p.   cm.
     "A Sarah Lazin book."
     ISBN 0-312-04517-4
          1. Motown Record Corporation. 2. Sound recording industry—United
States. I. Title
ml3790.f66   1990
781.66'09774'34–dc20   90–35545
                                                                      CIP
                                                                      MN

The text was set in Berthold Walbaum Standard and Futura by Mondo Typo, Los Angeles, California.
Color separations by Brite-Arts, Hong Kong
Printed and bound by Ringier America, New Berlin, Wisconsin

CONTENTS

his book began with the inspiration of a young, energetic Motown vice president, Traci Jordon. When Traci came across Motown's photography archives soon after she joined the company, she realized that she had discovered a treasure trove. Most of the photographs had been hidden away for years; many had never been published. As she and her associate, music critic Belma Johnson, began sorting through the huge and casually catalogued archives, they realized that publishing these photos would be a wonderful contribution to Motown's thirtieth-anniversary celebration, scheduled for 1990. That was less than two years away – a short time for such a complicated project.

Soon afterward, editor Marianne Partridge and myself met with Traci and Belma at Motown's offices overlooking Sunset Boulevard to discuss how such a book could be formed. The selection of the art director was critical to the book's success, and we were fortunate indeed when graphic designer Sheila Levrant de Bretteville agreed to join the project. Through her vision, creative energy, and drive, Sheila helped to shape the book and give it direction; through her innovative use of photography and lyrics, she gave it life and integrity. As the book's editor, Marianne, a long-time unabashed admirer of Motown, steeped herself in its music and history. The book's cohesiveness, from the selection of photographs to the writers' contributions, is the result of her guidance. She and Sheila worked together as an unparalleled team. Without their collaboration and dedication, this book would never have realized the original dream. Throughout, Jheryl Busby, president of Motown Records, served as the book's shepherd and protector.

Never did Jheryl help us more than when he introduced us to Georgia Ward and Faye Hale. These two dedicated Motown veterans not only drew on their own memories but contacted friends and acquaintances who also helped with the project. Through Georgia and Faye we found Janie Bradford, Beans Bowles, the Jamersons, and Maxine Powell, members of the Motown family who provided us with invaluable snapshots and information.

Ilene Cherna-Bellovin, the book's photo editor, led the search for photographs to supplement the Motown archives. With early assistance from Vikki Prudden, Ilene worked as a tireless investigator tracking down collectors worldwide. Tracye Saar helped to sort through the many photography collections on the West Coast and logged the thousands of images with a dedication that proved invaluable. We are deeply indebted to the many photographers who captured the various stages of Motown's evolution over the years and to the collectors who have treasured and saved their work, particularly Michael Ochs.

Special thanks must go to Vivian Chow and Jennifer Egger of the Sheila Studio, talented and tireless designers who performed above and beyond the call of duty. Joe Molloy of Mondo Typo also came through in the crunch. We are grateful to John Raymond and Andrea P. A. Belloli, our support editorial staff, who helped to get copy into shape under tight deadlines; to Holly George-Warren, who headed the research and fact-checking staff and who always adds immeasurably to any project of which she is a part; and particularly to Meg Jeffrey, who performed a myriad of services large and small. Thanks also to David Bianco, Joel Selvin, Patty Romanowski, Nelson George, Lynne Richardson, Jonathan Hyams, Matt

Spier, Sandy Choron, Ed Sturmer, Bob George, and the staff of the Archive of Contemporary Music.

We were fortunate to work with three very strong and knowledgeable writers. Elvis Mitchell and Motown grew up in Detroit together. While preparing his introduction, Elvis returned to his hometown neighborhood, the same one in which the fledgling record company developed, and his writing reflects these memories. Dave Marsh, who also grew up in Detroit, provided a critical discography re-evaluating the roll call of songs that have made Motown great; his love for the music is evident in his writing. Ben Fong-Torres worked under enormous deadline pressure to write the text and captions, which are imbued with grace and style. As *Rolling Stone*'s music editor through much of the seventies, Ben developed a unique understanding of Motown's history. We are grateful for his unending enthusiasm, knowledge, and energy.

The writers and the editorial and design staffs all relied heavily on the written record of Motown's history, most particularly David Bianco's comprehensive *Heat Wave: The Motown Fact Book* (Pierian Press). Other sources included Nelson George's *The Michael Jackson Story* (Dell) and *Where Did Our Love Go?* (St. Martin's Press); Peter Benjaminson's *The Story of Motown* (Grove); Gerri Hirshey's *Nowhere to Run* (Times Books); Dave Marsh's *The First Rock & Roll Confidential Report* (Pantheon) and *The Heart of Rock and Soul* (New American Library); David Ritz's *Divided Soul: The Life of Marvin Gaye* and, with Smokey Robinson, *Smokey* (both McGraw-Hill); Allan Slutsky/Dr. Licks's *Standing in the Shadows of Motown* (Hal Leonard); John Swenson's *Stevie Wonder* (Harper and Row); J. Randy Taraborrelli's *Call Her Miss Ross* (Carol) and *Motown: Hot Wax, City Cool & Solid Gold* (Dolphin); Don Waller's *The Motown Story* (Scribner's); and Patty Romanowski's collaborations with Otis Williams – *Temptations* (G. P. Putnam's) – and Mary Wilson – *Dreamgirl* (St. Martin's Press). Joel Whitburn's *Record Research* was, as always, enormously helpful.

We thank the Motown staff who gave us much-needed assistance and information on the company, especially the knowledgeable Miller London, Julie Moss, Mike Mitchell, Susan Wester, Ruth Burghardt, C. L. Merritt, Ellen Williams, Karen Sherlock, and Steven Meltzer. Many thanks also to Harry Anger, whose presence at Motown is most welcome.

This book would not have been done without the support of St. Martin's Press and the people there who believed in it from the beginning, especially Jim Fitzgerald but also Karen Gillis, Andy Carpenter, J. P. Olsen, and Amy Miller.

For his invaluable advice and counsel, we thank Larry Kenswil of MCA Records, who acted as friend and protector of this project through many difficult moments. We also are indebted to Lisa Riback of MCA Records; Susan Grode; Esther Gordy Edwards of The Motown Historical Museum; Lester Sill and Gloria Robertson of Jobete Publishing Co.; Suzanne de Passe and Suzanne Coston of Motown Productions; and Edna Anderson of the Gordy Company.

Finally, we must thank Berry Gordy, who not only gave us a terrific foreword but who gave us Motown itself. Thank you, Mr. Gordy, for keeping us dancing in the streets.

— Sarah Lazin

*W*HEN Jheryl Busby, president of Motown Records, asked me to write the foreword to this book I was busy at work on my autobiography and I told him I couldn't take time away from my own book to write something for another one. He was very patient with me and asked if I would just take a look at it anyway to see if I approved of the direction they were taking – if I would simply review the photographs and offer any comments, perhaps some thoughts. "After all," he said, "it all began with you – it was your dream."

Jheryl Busby is a very smart man. He knew that once I saw the photographs there was no way I could resist. Here I was toiling away on my computer, burning a hole in my brain struggling to remember, summon, and call upon now-faded memories in an attempt to bring to my future readers the truth of my life. And here it was right in front of my eyes – an exciting, remarkable, astonishing pictorial history of the golden days of Motown – my life!

Why didn't I think of this – using photographs to help me remember and relive those thrilling days of "yester year, yester me, yester you?"

This book is a powerful reminder of how much time has passed since the early days – so filled with hope and determination – pioneering days when none of us really knew what we were doing or where we were going. Oh, we knew the music and talent part

Founder of Motown
Records Berry Gordy:
"I was basically a dreamer
of love songs."

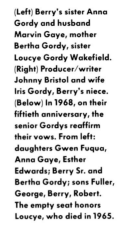

(Left) Berry's sister Anna Gordy and husband Marvin Gaye, mother Bertha Gordy, sister Loucye Gordy Wakefield. (Right) Producer/writer Johnny Bristol and wife Iris Gordy, Berry's niece. (Below) In 1968, on their fiftieth anniversary, the senior Gordys reaffirm their vows. From left: daughters Gwen Fuqua, Anna Gaye, Esther Edwards; Berry Sr. and Bertha Gordy; sons Fuller, George, Berry, Robert. The empty seat honors Loucye, who died in 1965.

Pride and joy: Marvin Gaye joined the Motown family in 1963 when he married Anna Gordy. "Anna and I were both hot characters with hot ambitions," Marvin said. "She was pushing me to be a champ." From left: Esther Edwards, Berry, Bertha Gordy, Gaye, Loucye Gordy Wakefield, with Anna in veil.

Berry celebrates with Anna and mother Bertha at the Sterling Ball (left), an annual charity event sponsored by Motown to raise funds for a Detroit scholarship program. Dancing in the living room (right): Brother Robert Gordy with wife Theresa and Bertha and Berry "Pops" Gordy, Sr., cut the rug. By 1965 the parties had moved to Gordy, Jr.'s three-story mansion on Boston Boulevard (below).

In a late sixties Christmas card Berry Gordy shows off the kids at their best. From left: Berry IV, Terry, Hazel, nephew Gregory; on the floor: Chico Ross, brother of Diana.

The best things in *life* are free

alright, but the other part – how to manage a business and take on the

responsibility for everything from signing and grooming the acts to promotion

and distribution of the product – was brand new to all of us.

I did not go to college. My classroom was

the world and there were no dress rehearsals. I have thought many times

of mistakes I made – particularly in the early days – due simply to just not

knowing better. I released a smash hit record on Mary Wells shortly before

her twenty-first birthday – shortly before she would legally be able to disaffirm

all contracts and move to another company – which she did. Even when I

knew better there were times when mistakes were just unavoidable.

Our loyalty to one another and to our goals

was so strong that the only reasonable description of that energy was

something beyond business and beyond contracts – it was the sticking together

that only happens in families. I ought to know since I was one of eight kids

myself, the lucky seventh. Fuller, Esther, Anna, Loucye, George, Gwen, and

Robert all worked at Motown along with Mother and Pop. You could find a

Gordy lurking in practically every department.

Though we did not coin the term ourselves,

the "Motown family" was not a description any of us took lightly. It was

how other people described us, because it was the impression we gave

other people. It doesn't matter what really accounted for our being perceived

as a family, but I can tell you we all believed that we were. We certainly

but you can give them to the *birds* and bees,

I need m o n e y

that's . . what I want

that's what I w a n t

that's . . what I want

that's what I w a n t

that's . . what I want

that's what I want

what I want

your love give me *such* a thrill

but your love don't *pay* my bills,

I need m o n e y

that's . . what I want

that's what I w a n t

that's . . what I want

that's what I w a n t

that's . . what I want

that's what I want

what I want

Money
By Berry Gordy
and Janie Bradford

Berry with Janie Bradford, a key figure in early Motown history who co-wrote "Money (That's What I Want)" with him. The song, recorded by Barrett Strong, was the eighth release on Tamla. Berry produced the record and pitched in background vocals.

fought and loved like one. We would never have accomplished as much if that spirit had not existed.

But, as with most families, some members decided to move on. Yet family roots are deep and connected and strong – our anniversary show, "Motown 25: Yesterday, Today, Forever," proved that. Although many early Motown members had indeed left, they returned to celebrate the truth of their beginnings, and, as with other great family reunions, it was an all too brief, emotionally charged event.

Sitting there, it was the first time I realized that Motown itself had become a legend, an institution, woven deeply into the fabric of American culture. Thirty years ago in Detroit none of us would have even dared to dream this could happen.

Over the years I have been called an entrepreneur, a mogul, a legend, a hero, a teacher, a super-star builder, a philosopher, a psychologist, a crook, a rip-off artist, a mafia underling – underling!? – all-around bad guy, all-around good guy – you name it.

What I am, however, is one who has never been hung up on labels, period. My policy was to never comment publicly on the bad or the good. My mother always told me that the best defense is a good offense. (A cliché, I know, but they work and I love 'em.) "Keep developing people," she'd say, "and getting hit records, and you'll be fine." And she was right. I was.

The impact of this book will be different for all those who come to it. Some will see it as a treasure of moments lived and now relived. For the dedicated Motown fan perhaps it reveals insight much deeper than what has been available up to now. Music lovers all over might just remember what was happening in their lives at that time. And to the completely uninitiated, it may only serve to illustrate the rate at which I lost my hair. For me, a picture in this book is worth not only a thousand words, but a thousand memories and emotions as well.

I was amazed at the fact that the new Motown did what I never thought to do: search for rare photographs, not only from the Motown Museum in Detroit, but from the many photographers, collectors, and fans all over the world. I even saw copies of photos from the library in my own home – when I thought I had the only copy.

I have developed a great love and appreciation for art, but few paintings can match the raw, real, unique moments captured in these photographs.

I, like many others, have my own personal, private memories and emotions about Motown. They're mine. And with this book, I will so enjoy seeing and feeling them again . . . and again.

—Berry Gordy

March 1990

THE hurtling steaminess of the Contours, with perspiration flying out of their freshly conked hair – like having the sweat knocked off them in the ring; the supercool precision of the Temptations, smoothly interlocking pistons wrapped in iridescent silk; the invigorating spunk-funk of Little Stevie Wonder, who seemed to be drunk on the crashing waves of applause which fanned out from the audience – these were all hypnotic parts of the Motortown Revue, which was, for me, all part of growing up in Detroit during the 1960s.

I especially recall two of the show's least mobile performers: Smokey Robinson, who tried halfheartedly to keep time but ended up just swaying and bouncing, communicating so much sheer joy that it didn't really matter that he wasn't a dancer; and another performer, who sang with his eyes closed, dangerously, magnetically self-assured. I remember guys muttering that he must really have thought he was something. I didn't know his songs very well, so I paid closer attention to his records after that. It was a long time before Marvin Gaye's seductive dazzle was fully embodied on record – but he was the coolest guy in the whole world.

Funnily enough, it was the men who got to me more. Of course, I was only six years old in 1963 (though even at that age I was stirred by something in Martha Reeves). But it was those guys, in their slim-goody neckties and gator shoes with gleaming finishes and points, who

became the symbol for breaking out of the neighborhood. For growing out of the inner city and reaching something better.

What I didn't realize, in those days when civil rights were new and strange (as compared to now, when apparently they're just strange), was that Motown was about assimilation. The Temptations and the Miracles, the Marvelettes and the Supremes were not making music like the records my parents listened to, like the Ray Charles songs that wafted out of the beauty salon down the street along with the scent of newly pressed hair. Motown was making the Sound of Young America, and it was paving a path to the promised land.

Even though Martha and the Vandellas' "Heat Wave," with its assaultive resonance, drew attention to the opportunities that evaded blacks, Motown nevertheless signaled a better way: If you took the advice of the old folks and worked twice as hard as the white man and completed college, then a richer, fuller life was yours for the asking. Berry Gordy, who grew up on the East Side, where I was born, had done it.

This came back to me recently when I went back to Detroit to visit the Motown Historical Museum, located at the original Hitsville, USA on West Grand Boulevard. There was another Motown office building in downtown Detroit, but that was used by the record company for only a few years before Gordy moved most of the operation to Los

The marvelous
Marvelettes get down;
Wanda Young sings lead
vocals with Gladys
Horton at left, and
Georgeanna Dobbins
on backup.

Angeles. In the 1970s, that empty building seemed to my friends and me – as we walked past it on our way to movies and concerts, with our Afros towering like elm tree foliage, our tough and velvety street jargon – like something from Stonehenge, a cold stone structure inhabited by a civilization of wizards and sorcerers a very long time ago. The West Grand Boulevard building, however, was where it all began, and for me, going back, it was like going back to your grandparents' house and discovering that history had taken place there. Standing in that tiny, remarkable place I realized that what Motown meant to me, more than anything else, was hunger, a ravenous need to prove equality and get social acceptance in these United States. More than anything, Motown wanted middle-class success, because it was the way to buy into the ideals of integration for which Lyndon Johnson's Great Society posted vacancy signs all over America.

Ironically, it wasn't what Motown's most fervent admirers – that is, its most fervent white admirers – wanted. They wanted to discover the kernel of truth in soul's Heart of Darkness, the easy, gospel-charged power that crackled like a distant thunderstorm in Levi Stubbs's delivery. This phenomenon is clearly depicted in all the accounts of the Supremes' meeting with the Beatles. The Supremes pulled themselves together in their best prim finery, no doubt smelling of Jungle Gardenia and dressed in gloves and pink suits with white piping and pillbox hats from some

approximation of the Jackie Kennedy collection. They couldn't have been farther from what John, Paul, George, and Ringo were anticipating. The Fab Four were ready for tough, sexy mamas who'd grab them by their Adam's apples and throw them roughly onto the grassy knolls of the Garden of Eden – sneaking the pale, eager Liverpudlians by the "No Whites Allowed" sign the Rolling Stones were trying to bully their way past ("O' course we got passes. 'Ey, Keef, show this bloke yer pass. . . ."). By analogy, the Beatles were expecting to recklessly eyeball the Tina Turner of the '84 "Private Dancer" tour, and the Supremes probably thought they'd sup tea and munch cucumber sandwiches with the sons of Richard Burton. They must've all been surprised to see that they were traveling past each other, trying to assume the others' cultural identity.

Eventually, though, the Supremes – and Diana Ross – did a much better job of stepping through the looking glass. What white-lipsticked white girl didn't pony in front of a mirror wearing white go-go boots and a fringed dress, lipsynching, "Come see about me . . . see 'boutcha ya baby?" The unregenerate ambition, the driving force behind Motown, was to put its songs, and its records, over to the biggest number of buyers possible. They succeeded by selling the exoticism of big-city soul to the suburbs everywhere.

As Barrett Strong sang, and Berry Gordy and Janie Bradford wrote, in 1959: "The best things in life are free, but you can give them to the birds and the bees. I need

This is an i n v i t a t i o n across the nation,

a chance for the folks to m e e t.

There'll be laughin', singin'

and music swingin',

and dancing

in the *street*.
dancin' in the streets

Philadelphia, P.A.,

Baltimore and D.C. now,

can't forget the Motor City,

a l l we need is music,
sweet sweet

sweet music,
sweet sweet music
there'll be music e v' r y w h e r e....
sweet...e v' r y w h e r e

money (that's what I want). . . . That's what I want." The unapologetic low throb and the jangling pulse of "Money (That's What I Want)" are vast and contain multitudes.

Gordy began in the music business as a songwriter, getting his material waxed by the original hardest-working-man-in-show-business, Jackie Wilson. Gordy's best known Wilson-sung lyric is probably "That's Why (I Love You So)," wherein Gordy meticulously builds up a litany of reasons for his true love. It's a simply stated piece, but as performed by Wilson, it's a sonnet delivered with the force of a right hook.

Both Wilson and Gordy boxed, and the fighter's nerviness was evident in each man. In the few public appearances of Gordy that I recall from my childhood, I remember vaguely an older cousin noting that Gordy moved like a pro fighter. At the time the only pro fighter I was familiar with was Cassius Clay, whose feathery grace was totally opposed to Gordy's low, lean, and intent stride; only later did I learn that Clay had the physical elegance of a swimmer. It was Gordy's defiant gait that seemed more appropriate to the task of boxing and, apparently, to the task of making records. To me, however, Gordy just looked like a man who knew exactly where he was going and how he was going to get there.

—*Elvis Mitchell*

Dancing in the Street
By William Stevenson,
Marvin Gaye and
Ivy Hunter

Detroit is the Motor City, and its auto plants provided a background for this early promotional photograph in which Martha and the Vandellas ride the assembly line for "Dancing in the Street." From left: Rosalyn Ashford, Martha Reeves, Betty Kelley.

*I*t is not enough to say that Berry Gordy was the man behind Motown. He was all around it: pulling it ahead; nursing it along; pushing, prodding, cracking the whip; doing whatever it took to turn the Motown Sound into the Sound of Young America.

He succeeded beyond his wildest dreams. In the years since he founded Motown, it has become the most famous record company in the world.

From the start Gordy fostered a family atmosphere around the Motown studios, which he called Hitsville, USA. For Gordy, family meant hard work, discipline, the willingness to be on call twenty-four hours a day, and a one-for-all philosophy. It only made sense. Gordy, after all, was one of eight children from a tightly knit family of loyal, hard workers. In the 1920s his father, Berry Gordy, Sr., grandson of a Georgia slave and her owner, had moved to Detroit, a city booming with the strength of the auto industry, a city of opportunity for blacks as well as whites. "Pops" wanted to

Through Motown's thirty-year history Berry Gordy (below) has been known as Berry Gordy, Jr., B.G., the Boss, and the Chairman, but to Marvin Gaye he was "the coolest dude I've ever met. This cat was serious."

At Hitsville, Berry serenades some of Detroit's finest singing, songwriting, and producing talent, including Holland-Dozier-Holland and the Primettes, who later became the Supremes.

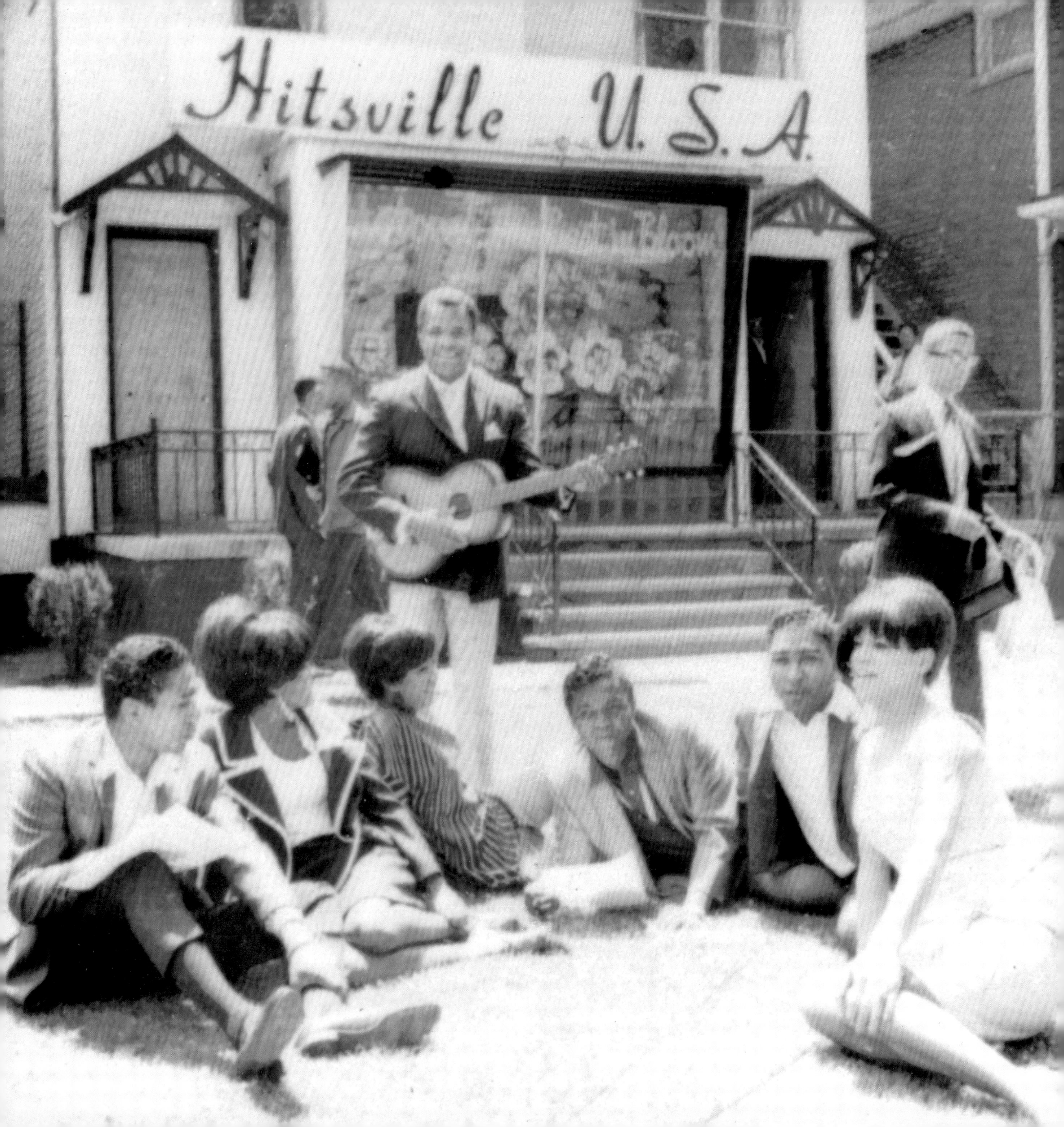
Hitsville U.S.A.

be his own boss. He and his wife, Bertha, owned and operated numerous small businesses in the Detroit area, and they instilled in their eight children an entrepreneurial message: If you work hard you can make it, and if you can make it on your own, all the better.

Berry Gordy, Jr., who was born in 1929 at the beginning of the Great Depression, at first did not seem to follow in his parents' successful footsteps. He began as a bantamweight boxer, did a stint in the army, and worked at the family businesses and on the Ford assembly line. He even tried his own business – a jazz record shop – but it lasted only two years. Along the way, he had a failed marriage and three children.

What Gordy most wanted to do was to make something out of the music he had begun to hear in his head. "I was basically a dreamer of love songs. . . . All I ever really wanted out of this business was to be a songwriter. I never got a rush like the rush I got when I wrote a hit."

Hot young songwriter Berry Gordy in 1960 with the man who sang his songs, Jackie Wilson. After "Reet Petite" came "Lonely Teardrops," "That's Why (I Love You So)," and "I'll Be Satisfied." (Right) Barrett Strong, who sang "Money," went on to become a Motown songwriter, collaborating with Norman Whitfield on such hits as "Cloud Nine," "I Can't Get Next to You," "War," and "I Heard It through the Grapevine."

Detroit singer Marv Johnson (above) helped Berry move from writer to producer on the 1959 record "Come to Me." (Left) From the Moonglows came Harvey Fuqua, at right: producer, talent scout, and future director of Motown Artists Development.

(Right) In a 1959 publicity campaign for a new release, "Snake Walk," promotion director Al Abrams dressed up in a turban and brought along a snake, terrifying Marv Johnson. The record wasn't a hit, but as Gordy, at far right, said, "We learned that no matter what you do to promote a record, it's what's in the groove that counts." Eddie Holland, at far left, as part of the songwriting team of Holland-Dozier-Holland, certainly knew what to put in the groove.

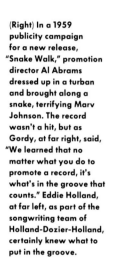

(Right) The rest of the H-D-H team is Lamont Dozier, at far right, and Brian Holland, at center, who pose with two other Motown powerhouses, William "Mickey" Stevenson and William "Smokey" Robinson, seated.

From the beginning he had good luck finding singers – and an audience – for his songs. Jackie Wilson, a Detroit ballad artist, recorded "Reet Petite," a song Gordy had written with Roquel "Billy" Davis, a boyfriend of his sister Gwen. In no time it hit the top of the R&B charts. With Davis and Gwen, Gordy wrote four more songs, including "Lonely Teardrops," that hit both the pop and R&B charts between 1957 and 1959.

But Gordy wasn't satisfied. As a songwriter he had no control over how his music was produced. By the time they became records, his songs often had become strangers to his ears. To gain more control he began to produce his own songs in 1957. One of his first productions was "Got a Job," an answer to a big hit by the Silhouettes called "Get a Job." The recording group on "Got a Job" was the Matadors, whose lead singer was another songwriter from Detroit, Smokey Robinson.

Without a label of his own, Gordy was forced to lease

And then she said

Just because you've become

a young man now,

momma

there's still some things

that you don't

understand now,

uh huh

Before you ask some girl

for her hand now,

uh huh

keep your freedom

for as long

as you can now.

uh huh

My mama told me,

You better shop around,

shop shop shop

oh yeah, you better

shop around.

In 1962 Smokey (holding the microphone) was among the performers at a fundraiser following an auto accident that turned the first Motortown Revue into tragedy, leaving a tour driver, Ed McFarland, Jr., dead and tour manager Thomas "Beans" Bowles hospitalized. Beans, on crutches, was a musician who became part of Motown's management division, International Talent Management, Inc. From left: Smokey flanked by Anna Gordy, Berry, Bill Murray (who, as "Winehead Willie," was emcee of the first Motortown Revues), Agnes and Beans Bowles, an unidentified musician, Esther Edwards, Ardenia Johnston (an assistant to Maxine Powell), Loucye Gordy Wakefield. After Beans complained that the young Motown performers needed polishing, Gordy created the Artists Development department. (Right) Berry and his first gold record, for "Shop Around." Not until the late seventies did Motown join the Recording Industry Association of America (RIAA), which audits record sales and certifies such awards. Until then Motown made do by spray-painting and framing its own gold records.

Shop Around
By Berry Gordy and William "Smokey" Robinson

Norman Whitfield (left) came to Motown hoping to be a songwriter. Berry gave him a job listening to records and running a newly created division, Quality Control. Whitfield went on to become one of Motown's most influential writers and producers with Gladys Knight and the Pips, Marvin Gaye, Edwin Starr, and, most of all, the Temptations.

(Far right) Joining Berry at the piano are, from left, Brenda Holloway, Georgeanna Dobbins, Katherine Anderson, Mary Wilson, Florence Ballard, Diana Ross, Iris Gordy, Gladys Horton, Wanda Young, Bobby Rogers, Little Stevie Wonder, and Kim Weston. (Above) At a session of Motown's "charm school," Maxine Powell, second from left, works with Florence Ballard, at far left, while an assistant and Mary Wilson look on. Wilson remembered Powell's stock opening phrase: "Young ladies always . . ." (Right) Powell in London, standing ready, near the gates of Buckingham Palace. (Left) Choker Campbell, on sax, organized the bands for the Motortown Revues.

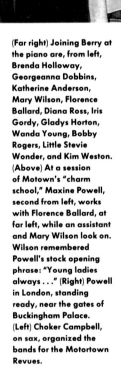

The leader of the Funk Brothers, Earl Van Dyke (right), started out playing bebop in Detroit clubs. Jam sessions resulted in a camaraderie known as "the Detroit way" that would be evident in the Snakepit, the recording studio at Hitsville, USA.

his records to other companies for distribution. He soon learned that independent producers were among the last to be paid for their work – if they were paid at all. It was Robinson who urged Gordy to set up his own label. "Why work for the man?" Robinson reasoned. "Why not *be* the man?"

Gordy, then thirty years old, embarked on his venture by turning to his family. Borrowing eight hundred dollars from his parents, he started Motown Records in a frame house at 2648 West Grand Boulevard in an ordinary black neighborhood and hired family members to become its first executives.

At the time, Detroit was a city alive with music and full of musicians, and it was that city's pool of talent which made up the core of the original Motown roster. From kids singing on street corners and in the corridors of housing projects came groups such as the Supremes and the Temptations. From veteran musicians and extraordinary young talents, working together as

session men, came the beat that became the Motown Sound.

Gordy commanded total control. He owned the rights to all the songs Motown recorded; he set up a management company for his artists and booked all of their concert and television appearances himself. He was tough and enjoyed competition.

At Motown, producers and writers vied to work with the hottest artists; producers and singers fought to have singles released; young singers scraped for their big chance; established singers worked to survive. Through it all, in those early days of Hitsville, USA, they loved what they were doing, and it showed. As Smokey Robinson recalled: "We just went at it with the idea that we were going to do something that made us happy, really... and we wanted it to be successful – of course."

(Above) Harvey Fuqua, in striped shirt, watches over the food; Maxine Powell sits patiently. (Left) Robert Gordy, with cap, shares a joke with the Miracles' Pete Moore, at left, while waiting in line at a barbeque. Behind Robert stands Diana Ross.

"In the early days," Earl Van Dyke recalled, "we were a family ... we had so many good times together. We had picnics, Christmas parties, or we just hung out." (Right) Berry with Berry Gordy, Sr., whom everyone at Motown called Pops.

Berry Gordy, ever the competitor, celebrates a victory in touch football at a Motown picnic with, from left, Marvin Gaye and songwriter Ron Miller. Smokey Robinson, wearing black, and Shorty Long join the winners.

(Above) At the same picnic: Marvin Gaye, facing the camera, and Barney Ales, with football, map out a play. Marvin had dreams of being a Detroit Lion; Ales headed sales and distribution. (Left) After the game Berry runs the barbeque pit as his sister Gwen tastes the ribs. Anna Gordy looks on.

MOTORTOWN REVUE

For Berry Gordy the Motortown Revue (later renamed the Motown Revue) was simply a way to expose his artists and sell more records. But it was also a way to show America what was going on in Detroit.

And so it was that, one morning in October 1962, Gordy spoke before an eager entourage made up of the best of Motown's artists. They were about to embark on a ten-week tour of what was known in those days as the chit'lin circuit, clubs and theaters mostly in the South and Midwest where black entertainers performed before mostly black audiences. The crown jewel of that circuit was New York's Apollo Theatre. If you made it there, you had arrived.

Gordy gave a pep talk – about how the performers were going to be representing Motown and how they had to behave like ladies and gentlemen – and sent them off. He was taking a gamble.

At the time powerful deejays such as Alan Freed and Dick Clark packaged pop acts

Just before the bus took off with the first Motortown Revue in October 1962, the performers, along with musicians and chaperones, posed in Studio A. "Look at us all," said Joe Billingslea of the Contours years later. "We had no idea in the world where we were *really* off to." The Contours are the six young men in the back row, at right; Marvin Gaye is third from left. In front of Marvin, next to a chaperone, are, from left, the four Marvelettes, Martha and the Vandellas, and the Supremes. The ten-week tour ended with a grueling ten-show stand at New York's Apollo Theatre.

On the road the Miracles perform for an enthusiastic young audience (left), but nothing could top playing the Apollo. "Sometimes," said Smokey, "I think heaven is stepping out at the Apollo on the heels of a hit." The Apollo Theatre was "the ultimate proving ground," he said. "If that hard-ass audience didn't like you, they'd let you know." (And a stagehand would come out with a long hook to encourage the act to leave.) Once, Smokey remembered, the audience brought them back for two encores of "Shop Around." The Supremes (right), performing at the Apollo in 1962 without benefit of a hit, also escaped that dreaded hook.

  Motortown Revue performers make their entrances from behind closed doors. (Small photos, from left) Tammi Terrell, Gladys Knight and the Pips, Martha and the Vandellas, ventriloquist Willie Tyler with his (not so) dummy, Lester.

for concerts and bus tours, but no record company before Motown had ever packaged its performers on tour itself.

This turned out to be a good move. Along with the records, the tours helped to give Motown an identifiable image – one that often needed polishing, however. At the Apollo a nervous Mary Wells told a baffled audience that she hoped she wouldn't "make a boo-boo."

The Detroiters had other reasons to be shaky. On this tour many of them had their first encounters with the segregated South their parents had moved to Detroit to escape.

In Birmingham, Alabama, the revue played before a racially mixed audience. As the performers began to board their bus after the performance, gunshots rang out in their direction. They piled onto the bus and raced out of town. Mary Wells remembered that first tour this way: "Me in my little Motown star bubble. All of a sudden everything kind of crushes."

Eddie Kendricks (above) handles a lead vocal for the Tempts, while Melvin Franklin, Paul Williams, David Ruffin (obscured), and Otis Williams do the Walk. (Left) Gladys Knight and the Pips: "We always tried to maintain a classy look," said Knight's cousin William Guest.

By the mid-sixties the Supremes (above) were in wigs and fringes. When the Motortown Revue played the Apollo, the girls were terrified. "We won the crowd over from the first minute," Mary Wilson recalled, "and came off the stage thrilled to death." Tammi Terrell (right), a performer since age eleven in Philadelphia, listens to enthusiastic audience response.

(Below right) A member of the comedy and dance troupe Kinfolks does his impression of Little Stevie while Martha Reeves watches. (Below left) The real Stevie.

(Above) Marvin Gaye at the Apollo with Martha and the Vandellas singing backup and Eddie "Bongo" Brown, who traveled with Marvin. Gaye found performing difficult. "The people were great to work with," he said about the shows, "but other than that, they were nightmares for me."

(Overleaf) The Miracles perform their "Mickey's Monkey" dance, with Claudette clapping in the background at Detroit's Fox Theater.

J UST as much as Berry," said Joe Billingslea of the Contours about Smokey Robinson, "that cat *is* Motown."

Besides having given Gordy the idea for starting his own record company, Robinson gave him the goods. In 1960 the group he had formed in high school – originally called the Matadors but renamed the Miracles at Gordy's suggestion – recorded "Shop Around." A song Gordy and Robinson co-wrote, it became the first Motown million-seller.

Smokey also produced records with the early Supremes, Marvin Gaye, the Marvelettes, the Temptations, and Mary Wells.

But most of all, Smokey gave Motown his songs. A romantic young man (it was poetic justice that he would fall in love with Claudette Rogers – cousin of a fellow Miracle, Bobby – and that she would join the group), he crafted Motown's cleverest, most enduring love songs. His writing crackled with wit and wonderment, with conflicts and paradoxes. His

Smokey credited much of his songwriting success to Berry Gordy, who looked at Smokey's first efforts and told him, "'Songs are more than rhymes'. . . . I kept doing those things Berry told me – you know, put a little story in the song to keep people's interest." Gordy sees the Miracles off to London in 1964. From left: Ronnie White, Bobby Rogers, Claudette Robinson, Pete Moore, Smokey Robinson, Gordy.

songs were sometimes blue
("Sweetness is only heartache's
camouflage/The love I saw in
you is just a mirage"). Some
burst with playful rhymes
("The Way You Do the Things
You Do"), others with plot
twists ("Two Lovers").

"They just come," he
has said of the approximately
fifteen hundred songs he's
written. In fact, they came
from a childhood filled with
good music. Growing up in
Detroit, he knew the music
of Sarah Vaughan (whose
singing he emulated) and of
Clyde McPhatter, the Moonglows, the Four Aims (later to
become the Four Tops), and
Jackie Wilson.

In performance
Robinson left the dancing to
his partners. But his songs, his
poignant near-falsetto, his
fresh-faced looks, his green
eyes, and his sleek physique
had the girls screaming.

As Linda Ronstadt
once said, "Wilson Pickett
looks like he'd jump right on
you, and then right off. Smokey
looks like he'd take weeks!"

Onstage (left), Smokey eyes Claudette. It was love at first sight, he said: "She was a cutie pie, a fox, flipping me out the first time I saw her." They were married in 1959, but Claudette stopped touring in 1964. After having numerous miscarriages, she finally accepted her doctor's advice to stay off the road, though she continued to record with the group until the late sixties. "Shop Around" made the Miracles sudden stars. Smokey Robinson remembered how, backstage at the Apollo (above right), "It looked like every kid from the audience was asking us for autographs."

Bill "Smokey" Robinson
Claudette
Bobby

Best Wishes
The Miracles

MIRACLES
Vocal Group

Personal Management
BERRY GORDY, JR.

The Miracles (above) were, from left, Bobby Rogers, who was the group's best dancer; Ronnie White, a fan of jazz and Ivy League clothes; and Pete "Pee Wee" Moore, who excelled at pool and other sports. Said Smokey: "We liked laughing together, we liked singing together — we even liked rehearsing." (Left) An early publicity photo.

From the beginning Motown rode high on the talents of Smokey Robinson, who not only wrote, produced, and sang "You've Really Got a Hold on Me" with the Miracles but also wrote and produced three Top Ten hits with Mary Wells: "The One Who Really Loves You," "You Beat Me to the Punch," and "Two Lovers." In just nine years, from 1961 to 1969, Smokey wrote or co-wrote forty-three songs that made the Top Forty pop charts, including the 1965 hit "Tracks of My Tears."

People say
I'm the *life* of the party
            'cause I tell
            a joke or two,
Although I might be l a u g h ing
loud and hearty
            deep inside
            I'm blue.
So take a *good* look at my face
You'll see my s m i l e
looks out of place.
            If you look *closer*,
            it's easy to trace
the tracks of my tears.
I need you.

The Tracks of My Tears
By William "Smokey"
Robinson, Warren Moore
and Marv Tarplin

Marvin Gaye had one
of the most effortlessly elegant
voices in pop music.

Born in Washington,
D.C., the son of a Pentecostal
minister, Gaye sang in his
father's church as a boy and
in doo-wop groups as a teenager. By the time he reached
Motown in 1961, after a stint in
the Moonglows, he was torn
between rhythm and blues and
the sophisticated pop of Nat
King Cole.

At first Gaye felt that
he fit perfectly into Gordy's
dream of making crossover
hits – songs that would sell not
only to black fans who bought
most R&B records but also to
the white audiences whose buying choices determined what
made the pop charts. "I figured
[I could be] another Johnny
Mathis," Gaye said. "Wow,
the world would love me!"

But when his first
album failed to sell, Gaye
repressed his dreams and
became "a good boy," serving
as a Motown session drummer
and pianist and co-writing
such songs as "Dancing in the
Street." Around Hitsville, he
was the picture of cool; his

Marvin Gaye's first
albums included a tribute
to Nat King Cole and a
collection of Broadway
show tunes. But while he
was willing to put on a
top hat and twirl a cane,
Marvin was continually
plagued by stage fright
and self-doubt. Along
with Mickey Stevenson
and Clarence Paul, he
wrote the 1963 hit "Hitch
Hike," which started a
nationwide dance craze.

"When I composed 'Pride and Joy,'" said Marvin, "I was head over heels in love with Anna. I just wrote what I felt about her and what she did for me. She was my pride and joy." Marvin with Anna Gordy and son Marvin Pentz Gaye III; Berry Gordy's son, Kennedy Gordy, sits on the floor. (Facing page) A baby boy and his dad at work.

and that's *why*

you are *my*

pride and joy.

And I'm telling the world

you're my

pride and joy,

pride and joy,

pride and joy,

I believe I'm your

baby boy,

baby boy,

baby boy.

Pride and Joy
By Norman Whitfield,
Marvin Gaye and
William Stevenson

I n s t e a d   I heard it through the grapevine.

good looks had the young girls swooning. But inside, he was in a panic. Always a shy performer who struggled through each concert, he also worried about not having scored a hit.

In 1963 Gaye married the boss's sister, the stunning Anna Gordy, seventeen years his senior. He might never be the king of Motown, he reasoned, but he could be a prince. When Anna chided Gaye for being stubborn, he turned the remark into his first modest hit, "Stubborn Kind of Fellow."

But through all the hits that followed – including his electrifying duets with women artists such as Tammi Terrell – and through his greatest triumph, "I Heard It through the Grapevine," which in 1968 became Motown's biggest hit record to date, Gaye remained unhappy, struggling with a family situation he found increasingly stifling. "I wanted to get into the top echelon of show business without paying all the dues," he said. But of course, he paid his share.

Marvin, who changed his surname from Gay to Gaye when he became a performer, was called Gates around Hitsville and Dad by Smokey Robinson. In 1968 he had no idea that "I Heard It through the Grapevine" would become a hit. In fact, he said, "I had no idea it would be released." On further reflection its success seemed preordained. His mother's father, he remembered, once told her "that her son would be responsible for part of her success and that some of his fortune [lay] under the grapevines." Marvin's comment: "I think that's ironic."

Not much longer

would you be mine.

Oh, I heard it

through the grapevine.

And I'm just about to

l o s e my mind.

Honey, honey oh yeah.

I heard it

through the grapevine

not much longer

would you be mine

b a b y

**I Heard It through
the Grapevine**
By Norman Whitfield
and Barrett Strong

'Cause baby there ain't no mountain h i g h enough

Ain't No Mountain High Enough
By Nickolas Ashford and Valerie Simpson

Tammi Terrell is best remembered for her duets with Marvin Gaye on the songs "Ain't No Mountain High Enough," "Your Precious Love," and "Ain't Nothing Like the Real Thing." They were truly in sync. "Tammi's singing style was perfectly suited to mine," remembered Marvin. "We created two characters, two lovers, and let them sing to one another. While we were singing, we were in love. The vibe was incredible. But when the music ended, we kissed each other on the cheek and said good-bye." In 1967, onstage, Terrell collapsed in Gaye's arms. Following a series of operations for a brain tumor, she died in 1970. She was twenty-four. After her death Marvin refused to sing in public for several years. "In my heart I could no longer pretend to sing love songs for people," he said.

At Motown's peak, said Freddie Gorman of the Originals, "Everybody was buying Cadillacs. It was *the* thing to do to be prestigious. There'd be all these Cadillacs all lined up in front of Hitsville. Every time a producer or a writer got a Number One [hit], he'd run out and buy a Cadillac that was better than the one bought by the last producer or writer." Marvin, who earned his as a producer, a writer, and a performer, craved broad-based acceptance but feared that he was selling out.

Downstairs at Hitsville, USA was a converted basement known as the Snakepit where the hits were made. This was the perfect name for the tiny studio and the clashing egos who toiled there.

At all hours of the day or night Motown's singers, musicians, and instruments, including a concert grand piano, fought for space. Lead singers crammed into a cubicle the size of a phone booth.

They didn't have loads of equipment – musicians heard their music blasted out of one large speaker on the far basement wall – Gordy and his engineers were innovative with what they had. Motown was one of the first labels to record on eight tracks, allowing instrumentation and vocals to be laid down separately.

The music was certainly loud enough. To put a stop to neighbors' complaints, Gordy was forced to buy up several adjoining houses.

Despite the noise and the crowding, the Snakepit worked – for out of it came the Motown Sound, a phenomenon

The process of creating the Motown Sound ranged from the meticulously orchestrated – arranger Gil Askey (left) conducts a recording session – to a jam session with Stevie Wonder on drums (right). Playing with Stevie is songwriter Clarence Paul on tambourine and Eddie "Bongo" Brown. Motown, Stevie recalled, "was like a music store with all kinds of toys – instruments for me to play."

which, along with the Beatles
and the British Invasion,
dominated pop music in the
mid-sixties.

By 1966 three out of
every four Motown releases
were making the pop charts,
a far higher average than for
any other company.

Few have succeeded
in characterizing the specific
yet wide-ranging music that
comprised the Motown Sound.
Even Gordy had to fall back
on a one-liner of sorts when
asked to do this: "Rats,
roaches, love, and guts."

Critics have often
focused on Motown's compel-
ling lyrics as the source of its
magic. Gordy certainly kept at
his songwriters, urging them
to tell immediate, engaging
stories. But many musicians
feel that the propulsive bass
and pronounced rhythms were
the keys to the Motown Sound.

As Isaac Hayes, who
then was recording for Stax,
the Memphis R&B label,
noted: "It was the standard
joke with blacks, that whites
. . . you know – ain't got that
rhythm. What Motown did was
very smart. They beat the kids

The various Funk
Brothers, as vital as
they were to the
Motown Sound, were
largely unknown to
the public. As Stevie
Wonder put it, "People
weren't really that
interested in the musicians."
(Left) Stevie fronts Robert
White, on guitar,
Hank Cosby, and James
Jamerson, on bass.
(Right) Bongo Brown,
Uriel Jones, on drums,
and Jamerson, on guitar,
at a nightclub gig.

Earl Van Dyke, leader of Motown's session musicians, estimated that the Funk Brothers were behind the scenes on recordings that sold 250 million copies. (Left) Earl, seated at his piano, is flanked by, from left, White, Danny Turner, Jones, Jamerson, and popular disc jockey Martha Jean (aka "The Queen"). (Right) Jamerson, Hunter, Cosby; at front, from left, Benny Benjamin, Larry Veeder, Mike Terry.

over the head with it. That
wasn't soulful to us at Stax, but
baby, it sold."

The Motown Sound
also involved some downright
homey inventions. "Money"
co-writer Janie Bradford
recalled: "It didn't matter how
it sounded; it was all about
how it felt. We'd make all
kinds of effects on records,
shaking beans in a jar, whip-
ping chains, like on 'Nowhere
to Run,' clapping boards,
whatever it took."

More than anything,
it took a team of session musicians known as the Funk
Brothers. The original crew
included Benny Benjamin on
drums, James Jamerson on
bass, Eddie Willis and Joe
Messina on guitars, bandleader
Earl Van Dyke and Johnny
Griffith on keyboards, and
Jack Ashford on percussion.

The main drivers
were Jamerson and Benjamin.
Gordy has called Jamerson
"an incomparable bass player
who pumped lifeblood into
hundreds of our Motown hit
records." As for Benjamin,
Stevie Wonder has said: "Just
listen to all the old hits,

Songwriter Frank Wilson works out a song for Chris Clark while Hal Davis watches. Clark, one of the few white artists at Motown in the early days, later became an executive for the company and worked on the screenplay for *Lady Sings the Blues*. Wilson wrote for the Supremes and Brenda Holloway, among others, while Hal Davis worked with Thelma Houston, Michael Jackson, and the Jackson 5.

The blackboard lists a typical schedule of rehearsals and lessons at Hitsville, where Motown's music-makers worked not only around the clock but wherever there was enough space in which to squeeze a piano and a few performers. Tammi Terrell (left) practices a tune with arranger Johnny Allen, at piano, and Maurice King, Artists Development director. Maxine Powell, on the phone, listens while she works. On what must have been a cold day in Detroit in 1964, members of the Temptations (right) listen and sing along to a new song. From right: Paul Williams, Otis Williams, David Ruffin, Melvin Franklin. Eddie Kendricks, at far left, sings lead while Johnny Allen plays and Harvey Fuqua conducts.

'My World Is Empty without You' and 'This Old Heart of Mine'. . . . On 'The Girl's Alright with Me,' the drums would just **POP**!"

Though Gordy and Smokey Robinson provided some of Motown's first, best songs, Berry was always looking for new talent. In Detroit it was easy to find songwriters who knew, or could learn, how to bring songs to life.

The roll call began with Brian Holland, Lamont Dozier, and Eddie Holland, who worked together and in combination with others, providing the Supremes with their first fifteen hit singles. Other major contributors were William "Mickey" Stevenson, Norman Whitfield, Hank Cosby, Barrett Strong, Ivy Hunter, Johnny Bristol, Sylvia Moy, Frank Wilson, Ron Miller, and Al Cleveland (who, with Pete Moore and guitarist Marv Tarplin, often wrote songs with Robinson). Clarence Paul worked with the young Stevie Wonder, and Nick Ashford and Valerie Simpson provided tunes for Marvin Gaye and Tammi

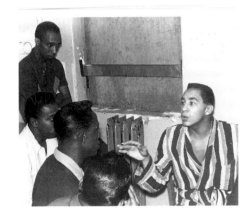

Smokey pitches a new song, entitled "My Girl," to the Temptations backstage at the Apollo; Miracle Ronnie White, at left, listens in. Tempt Otis Williams remembered: "I said, 'That might be something.'" It was the Tempts' first Number One hit, in 1965. The Four Tops (below) make a basement tape while choreographer Cholly Atkins, the lean machine (above right), works out a routine.

Cholly Atkins was demanding, as Katherine Anderson of the Marvelettes remembered: "We would work with Cholly sometimes for hours. I mean, you wouldn't feel like fooling with anybody else, because by the time Cholly got through beatin' it into you, you were done, you know? But every artist had to attend these classes, so when we went out, we went out as a finished product." Here Atkins rehearses Otis Williams, Paul Williams, a few Marvelettes, and the Temptations.

Terrell's duets and for
Diana Ross.

Motown artists may
have begun by playing the
chit'lin circuit, but Gordy was
determined that they ulti-
mately would be able to play
the world's finest supper clubs.
To train them to fulfill their
destinies, he created Motown's
Artists Development division
in 1964.

Motown U., as it was
called, hired seasoned
performers as teachers. Cholly
Atkins, half of the renowned
forties dance team Coles and
Atkins, designed and taught
dance steps to all the groups.

Bandleader Maurice
King – whose house band at
Detroit's Flame Show Bar
had worked with every major
black act – helped Motown
performers take their hits from
the studio to the stage.

Motowners also
learned how to act offstage.
Modeling school owner Maxine
Powell taught Motown's girls
how to walk, sit, and talk.
"We were training them for
Buckingham Palace and the
White House," she said. And
she was right.

(Above) Berry gives some
apparently astounding
news to, from left, singer
Barbara McNair,
producer Mickey Gentile,
and songwriter/producer
Mickey Stevenson. (Left)
Smokey, Berry, and Diana
listen with rapt attention
as Mary Wilson addresses
a meeting in Studio A.
(Below) A member of the
Vancouvers gives the
high sign.

Berry with older brother George (right), considered a straight arrow in the Gordy family. It was George, along with Mickey Stevenson, who came up with the idea of having balladeer Marvin Gaye cut a dance tune in 1962. George and Mickey wrote the song with Marvin, and the result, "Stubborn Kind of Fellow," was Marvin's first hit.

Smokey Robinson (above), a master at both sides of the microphone, is flanked by songwriter Al Cleveland (in hat) and engineer Bob Gratts. Cleveland is credited by Smokey with inspiring a hit song when, in a Detroit department store, he mangled a common expression and came up with "I second that emotion." (Right) Gaye listens to playbacks with producers Marc Jordan and, at right, Hal Davis at a recording session for his *Hello Broadway* album.

Until Motown, in Detroit, there were three big careers for a black girl," said Mary Wells. "Babies, the factories, or day work."

At age twelve Mary was doing day work, scrubbing floors by her mother's side. But Mary's mother had taught her independence. So, at seventeen, Wells marched into Motown hoping to sell a song, "Bye Bye Baby," which she'd written with Jackie Wilson in mind. Berry Gordy liked the wispy-voiced Wells, asked *her* to sing it, and signed her. The song was on the charts for almost three months.

Mary was the company's first female star. Beginning with "The One Who Really Loves You," she had three Top Ten songs in 1962. Two years later she was on tour with the Beatles.

At the height of her meteoric career Wells left Motown, claiming that her contract was too confining. Years later she confessed that she was surprised that other companies were not run with the same family atmosphere.

In a time of feisty girl groups, Berry liked the way Mary Wells could deliver a tune softly, with sophistication. Smokey provided her with "Two Lovers," in which Wells, sounding innocent and wicked at the same time, told about her two boyfriends, one good, one bad, and how "I love them both the same." The two turned out to be one man with a split personality.

Nothing you could s a y could tear me away

from my guy.

Nothing you could do 'cause I'm stuck like g l u e

to my guy.

My Guy
By William "Smokey"
Robinson

Backstage at the Apollo
(left), Mary gets a visit
from choreographer
Cholly Atkins. "We were
all kids on those big
tours," she said, "just a
bunch of kids that cared
about each other, havin'
fun. Growin' up together.
Those were our years of
higher education."
Onstage she puts her
training to work.

CONTOURS

ᖴOR Berry Gordy the ideal male group at Motown sang and danced harmonically and exuded elegance and class. The Contours were not that group.

"We were the best dancers, that's the truth," said Joe Billingslea. "We did splits, jumped through each other's legs, dove headfirst, all that stuff. People would *scream*."

When the Contours performed "First I Look at the Purse," group member Council Gay remembered, women threw their handbags onto the stage. But when the Contours auditioned for Gordy in 1961, he initially rejected them. It was only as a favor to Jackie Wilson, a cousin of Contour Hubert Johnson, that he signed them.

And they got their first hit only because the Temptations were late for a session. Gordy handed the Contours the song, saying, "Let's see if you guys can do it."

They could, and "Do You Love Me" hit Number Three in 1962.

You broke my heart, 'cause I couldn't dance.
You didn't *even* want me around.
But now I'm back to let you know
I can *really* shake 'em down. . . .

Do you **love** *me?*

Do You Love Me
By Berry Gordy

The Contours look for the purse (left); Billy Gordon gets down while Sylvester Potts sings. During this performance at Detroit's Twenty Grand Club (right), Temptation Dennis Edwards, second from left, joins the Contours.

*I*T took a blind ten-year-old named Stevland Morris to break the mold at Motown.

Signing with the company in 1960, Little Stevie Wonder – as he was promptly renamed by Berry Gordy – gave the company its first self-contained performer: singer, musician, and, later, song-writer and producer.

Born in Saginaw, Michigan, and raised in Detroit, Stevie was never allowed to be limited by his blindness. He remembered hopping barn roofs with his brothers, playing around with girls, and getting plenty of "ironing cord whippings" because of his rambunctious-ness. Most of all, he remem-bered listening to music on the radio. At age nine he began singing and playing harmonica. A born mimic, Stevie staged front-porch performances, dazzling family and neighbors with shows he and a friend put together.

After a family friend, the brother of the Miracles' Ronnie White, brought the young star in for an audition at Hitsville, Stevie became a

In the early Motortown Revues, Little Stevie opened – and promptly stole – the shows. He'd drop to one knee and then to the floor, singing "A little bit softer now" until he was whispering, while the musicians would bring the music down lower and lower; suddenly, he'd reverse into "A little bit louder now," until the band was driving full-throttle and the crowd was half-mad. And then he'd leave, sometimes having to be carried offstage by Motown's Clarence Paul.

company mascot – and a student, learning drumming from Funk Brother Benny Benjamin.

Within a year Stevie was in the studio. But even before his first record, he was a hit in the Motortown Revue. As an opening act he would tear from one instrument to another, working the crowds with his energy, especially with "Fingertips," his first hit song. An album built around his performances gave Motown its first Number One album, in 1963.

By 1965 Stevie's musical interests had ranged far beyond the Motown Sound. He was listening to Bob Dylan and the Beatles. In 1966 he recorded Dylan's antiwar song "Blowin' in the Wind." "I just said, 'Why can't I?'" he explained. "So many people have categorized me, 'Stevie Wonder, soul artist.' I just wanted to do something else. I don't want to stay in one key all the time."

Everybody sing *yeah*,

YEAH,

say *yeah*,

YEAH,

say *yeah*,

YEAH,

yeah,

YEAH,

y e a h . What key?

What key?

Fingertips (Part 2)
By Clarence Paul and
Henry Cosby

"I loved to play jokes on everyone," said Stevie about his early times at Motown. Mimicking Berry Gordy, he'd call an employee "and say things like, 'This is Berry and I want you to go get Stevie that tape recorder right away. . . . I'm sure he'll get it back to us in a few days.' After they fell for this stunt about three times and never got the tape recorder back, they gave me a recorder as a belated birthday present." Conferring with Gordy (below) before a show.

Stevie with Clarence Paul (right), staff songwriter and producer who performed with him on records and on stage. Paul was also the arranger and conductor when Stevie was backed by a big band, and Stevie credits him with some of his more adventurous musical travels. "We would work out tunes [by other groups], ridin' in cars in England around '65," Stevie remembered.

OTOWN was no civil rights organization, and Berry Gordy was no Martin Luther King, Jr. – though the two men were friends, and Gordy contributed to King's work. But by making a success of the first black-owned enterprise of its kind, Gordy sent out vital messages in so many words – and in music.

It was ironic, then, that when the riots of 1967 set Detroit on fire, Motown was one of their victims. After the riots, the company relocated to a downtown office building. By 1972 Motown officially had moved to Los Angeles.

Around America, however, Motown was a healing force. The early Motortown Revues often broke down racial barriers, performing before the first integrated audiences in some parts of the country. Singer Ruben Guevera noted Motown's power to unite conflicting racial groups: "Whether it was Marvin Gaye or Mary Wells, it sounded good at the end of a day of hard work or no work, regardless of the color of your skin."

At Motown, Dr. Martin Luther King, Jr., was more than an inspiration; he was part of its roster. On the Gordy label, Motown issued a single of King's "I Have a Dream" speech and the album *The Great March to Freedom* in 1963, the year before the federal Civil Rights Act was passed. Gordy presents King (below) with the album while Lena Horne watches. King speaks before enormous Detroit crowds (left and right). On Black Forum, a short-lived subsidiary label for spoken-word recordings, the company released Dr. King's speech "Why I Oppose the War in Vietnam" on an album of the same name in 1970, two years after his assassination.

Despite all of the professional talent Gordy brought to Hitsville, it was at a high school talent contest that Motown found the group that gave the label its first Number One record.

The Marvelettes (originally the Marvels), who won the chance for a Motown audition, even provided their own song, worked up overnight by group member Georgeanna Dobbins.

The song was "Please Mr. Postman." Depending on how much attention you're paying, it begins with either "Boink!" or "Wait!" Either way, it's a perfect pop tart from this quintessential girl group. The Marvelettes were young, singing for the fun of it, and unpolished by Artists Development.

At Hitsville the classic success story involved the secretaries, many of whom were really singers looking for a break, but the Marvelettes were so early in the game that one member pulled a twist. In 1962 Dobbins left the group . . . to become a secretary at Motown.

The Marvelettes hit big in 1961 with "Please Mr. Postman," then hit not so big with the calculated follow-up, "Twistin' Postman." But they rebounded with "Playboy" and "Beechwood 4-5789" in 1962 and "Too Many Fish in the Sea" in 1964. (Left) Gladys Horton sings lead with Katherine Anderson, at left, and Wanda Young. (Right) By 1969 Ann Bogan, at right, had replaced Gladys.

The original Marvelettes
were a quintet and
included Juanita Cowart
(not pictured),
who left after
"Please Mr. Postman," and
Georgeanna Dobbins,
third from left. At left,
Katherine and Wanda
dance it up; at right,
Gladys shakes it down.
After the R&B smash
"Danger, Heartbreak Dead
Ahead" in 1965,
the remaining
Marvelettes hooked up
with Smokey Robinson,
who wrote and produced
"Don't Mess with Bill,"
"The Hunter Gets Captured
by the Game," and "My
Baby Must Be a
Magician." Smokey said
he didn't write "Bill"
about himself. "I just liked
the way the name sung,"
he said.

WAIT

Oh yes wait a minute Mr. Postman

WAIT

w a i t Mr. Postman

Please Mr. Postman look and see . . .

Oh y e a h

is there a letter in your bag for me?

Please, please Mr. P o s t m a n

You know it's been a long, long time

Oh y e a h

since I heard from that boyfriend of mine.

Please Mr. Postman
By Brian Holland, Robert
Bateman, Freddie
Gorman, Georgeanna
Dobbins and
William Garrett

MARTHA
&
THE VANDELLAS

At New York's Shea
Stadium in 1966
Martha chats with a
pair of Miracles. With
Holland-Dozier-Holland,
Martha and the Vandellas
scored with "Come and
Get These Memories,"
"Heat Wave," and
"Quicksand" in 1963;
"Live Wire" in 1964;
"Nowhere to Run" in 1965;
"I'm Ready for Love" in
1966; and "Jimmy Mack"
in 1967.

ARTHA Reeves was only four years old when she felt her first heat wave.

After attending a church where the featured soloist, Della Reese, delivered a searing "I Hear the Thunder," Reeves knew what she had to do. By the time she was a teenager she had formed her own girl group, the Del-Phis.

And when Motown refused them an audition, Reeves simply got a job there as a secretary. "I worked two weeks for nothing, I wanted to be there so much."

Soon she and her group, which changed its name first to the Vels and then to the Vandellas, had worked their way into Studio A, adding hand claps and vocals to Marvin Gaye's first recordings.

Reeves sounded the way she acted – bold and unafraid to sweat. Her hot, cutting voice was made for songs such as "Heat Wave" and "Quicksand," songs she said were based on the Charleston. Maybe, but make no mistake: Their roots are in a church where they believe in the gospel of the heat.

Nowhere to *run* to, b a b y,

nowhere to *h i d e*.

Got nowhere to run to, baby,

nowhere to *h i d e*.

Nowhere to Run
By Eddie Holland,
Lamont Dozier and
Brian Holland

Martha Reeves remembered what she and her group were doing when the 1967 riots broke out in Detroit: They were singing "Dancing in the Street" onstage there. When she heard later that the song, written by Marvin Gaye and Mickey Stevenson, was described as a call to riot, Martha was shocked. "My lord," she said, "it was a *party* song!" (Below) From right: Martha performs with Betty Kelley and Rosalyn Ashford; (right) the girls at the Twenty Grand Club, with Beans Bowles playing the horn. (Left) Martha waits while the Vandellas play cards backstage.

VELVELETTES

$\mathcal{A}$LTHOUGH Motown originally was called the Motown Record Corporation, its first label was Tammie, named by Gordy after a song from Debbie Reynolds's movie *Tammy*, which he'd liked. Tammie, which became Tamla, was followed in 1960 by the Motown label.

As he began signing new talent, Gordy created new labels. In 1961 came Miracle, with its double-edged slogan, "If It's a Hit, It's a Miracle." In 1962 Miracle was replaced by Gordy Records. That same year Motown also added Mel-O-Dy and VIP Records (home of the Velvelettes, who had one hit, the 1964 burner "Needle in a Haystack").

Gordy's sister Gwen and her husband, Moonglow Harvey Fuqua, had formed independent labels – Anna, Harvey, and Tri-Phi – which were absorbed into Motown when the couple began working at Hitsville. By 1964 Motown also was issuing records on the Soul and Workshop Jazz labels.

With subsidiary labels Gordy could avoid overloading any one company with artists.

The Velvelettes, from Kalamazoo, Michigan, had only one pop hit, "Needle in a Haystack" in 1964. Founding member Carolyn "Cal" Gill explained: "We were not as hungry for stardom as the other girl groups. We came from reasonably secure backgrounds . . . so our appetite to make a lot of money was not as intense as other girl groups at Motown."

Tell 'em 'bout the f u n c t i o n
at the j u n c t i o n
Tell 'em that they'd better
c o m e o n right now.

Function at the Junction
By Eddie Holland and
Frederick Long

He could place acts on some labels specializing in subcategories of music. And he could appease employees.

Workshop Jazz was created at the request of William "Mickey" Stevenson, who was in charge of signing and overseeing musicians, most of whom came from jazz backgrounds. Playing Motown's pop music made them comparatively good money, but Workshop Jazz gave Stevenson a competitive edge over other record companies eager to snatch Snakepit talent.

Motown won a Grammy with the Black Forum label, for the spoken-word album *Why I Oppose the War in Vietnam.*

When critics suggested that Motown's productions were in danger of getting too smooth, Gordy didn't tamper with his formula; he merely added to it. Soul Records came about when he realized that new markets were opening up for a more basic form of black music now called soul. The new label became a home for Gladys Knight and the Pips and a few other, smaller gems.

Frederick Long was five-feet-one and thus Shorty. He came to Motown as part of its acquisition of Tri-Phi Records. His last hit, "Here Comes the Judge," was inspired by a routine on "Rowan and Martin's Laugh-In."

*J*IMMY Ruffin didn't possess all the vocal textures of his younger brother David (who sang with the Temptations), but he had enough to give Soul Records a Top Ten hit with "What Becomes of the Broken-hearted" in 1966.

The song was as deeply felt as it sounded. "My career wasn't doing well," he said. "I was hungry . . . depressed. I interpreted [the song] like a person who was lost . . . looking for a ray of hope."

Ruffin never matched that first hit, but he did well in England, where, in 1971, he finished second in a musical poll, just behind Elvis Presley.

Soul's first hit artist was a sax man, Autrey DeWalt, Jr., who, as Junior Walker, led his All Stars through a circuit of Midwestern bars and clubs before joining the Motown family by way of Harvey Fuqua. In 1965 Walker's own composition "Shotgun" hit Number Four on the pop charts. Holland-Dozier-Holland gave him his next big hits, "(I'm a) Road Runner" and "How Sweet It Is (To Be Loved by You)."

Walker, who prided himself on his gutbucket sound and who never considered himself a singer, almost took offense when, in 1968, producer/songwriter Johnny Bristol offered him a ballad, "What Does It Take (To Win Your Love)." The next year, when Bristol pushed the song at him again, Walker told him, "Man, this ain't my bag." But Bristol persisted, and Walker wound up with another Number Four hit.

Along with the Contours, Shorty Long was one of Motown's most funky and frenetic performers. His "Devil with the Blue Dress" was the first Soul Records single. Long, who died in a boating accident in 1969, peaked in 1968 with the funky "Here Comes the Judge."

What becomes of the b r o k e n h e a r t e d, who had love that's now d e p a r t e d ?

What Becomes of the Brokenhearted
By James Dean, Paul Riser and William Weatherspoon

Jimmy Ruffin reaches out. His biggest year at Motown was 1966, when both "What Becomes of the Brokenhearted" and "I've Passed This Way Before" reached the Top Twenty.

I said **shot** g u n.

Shoot 'em 'fore he

run n o w .

Do the jerk b a b y .

Do the jerk now.

Shotgun
By Autry DeWalt

Junior Walker was at a
club in 1965 watching
kids doing a new dance.
When he asked one
dancer for the name of
the new step, he was told,
"It's the Shotgun, but we
need a song for it." Junior
got busy and, with Berry
Gordy producing, came
up with a hit.

𝒜MONG the women of Motown, the basis for so many projects-to-riches stories, Brenda Holloway's story most resembles a fairy-tale. She was mopping the floor in the kitchen of her home in Watts, daydreaming about recording for Motown, when she heard that the company would be represented at a deejays' convention in Los Angeles. Holloway showed up at the convention in a tight, gold lamé pantsuit with matching shoes and an entourage made up of her mother and a close friend. When a deejay, convinced that she must be a star, asked her to perform, she sang along with a Mary Wells record. As fate would have it, Berry Gordy was there and liked what he heard – and what he saw.

With Motown, Holloway had several hits, the biggest being her first, "Every Little Bit Hurts," in 1964.

Brenda Holloway (left) was the only female vocalist to accompany the Beatles on their 1965 world tour. In that same year Kim Weston (right) toured England with the Kinks and Gerry and the Pacemakers.

𝒦IM Weston, a Detroit
native who was discovered by
a cousin of Brian and Eddie
Holland, had her greatest
success in duet with Marvin
Gaye. "It Takes Two,"
co-written and produced by her
husband, Mickey Stevenson,
hit the Top Twenty in 1967.

A fine solo singer
and performer, Weston had a
modest hit in 1965 with her
version of "Take Me in Your
Arms (Rock Me a Little
While)" and is well represented in a duet album with Gaye,
Take Two.

Motown had its share
of artists who made more
music than money. And
although most of them were
fresh off the streets, there were
a number of seasoned performers who simply didn't click
with the Motown Sound – or
didn't click often enough.

THE Isley Brothers had their biggest hits outside Motown, both before – with "Shout" and "Twist and Shout" – and after – with "It's Your Thing." But at Motown in the mid-sixties, Ronald, Rudolph, and O'Kelly Isley did score with a Holland-Dozier-Holland song, "This Old Heart of Mine (Is Weak for You)."

The Monitors, who joined Motown's VIP label in 1965, issued only a half dozen records. But, for member Richard Street, the group was a stepping-stone back into the Temptations.

Street had founded the Distants with childhood friend Melvin Franklin and Otis Williams. Shortly after Street dropped out, the Distants merged with members of the Primes to become the Temptations.

Street caught up with the Tempts in 1971, joining just in time to make a run of hit records for that group. With the Monitors he had made none at all. The closest had been "Greetings (This Is Uncle Sam)," which sounded timely in 1966. It was actually a

The Isley Brothers – from left, O'Kelly, Ronald, and Rudolph – did better away from Motown. The Monitors (right) didn't have much luck anywhere. Their 1965 lineup included, from left, Warren Harris, Sandra Fagin, and, at the second microphone, future Temptations member Richard Street.

remake of a 1961 record by another Motown group, the Valadiers. The Monitors managed to squeeze into the Number 100 spot for a week, and then their moment was over.

Though the Originals formed in 1966, the individual members had worked at Hitsville from its earliest days. The group paid its dues by singing backup for Marvin Gaye, Jimmy Ruffin, Stevie Wonder, and other Motown artists.

In 1969 the Originals hit the Top Twenty with "Baby, I'm for Real," a song Gaye had written.

The members of the Elgins also were part of early Motown; lead singer Saundra Mallett cut a Tamla single, with the Vandellas on backup, in 1962, and the guys – Cleo "Duke" Miller, Johnny Dawson, and Robert Fleming – also recorded for Tamla as the Downbeats. In 1966 they came together as the Elgins for a brief fling with success: Two excellent singles, "Darling Baby" and "Heaven Must Have Sent You," reached the Top Ten of the R&B surveys.

The Spinners should have been perfect for Motown. They were from Detroit, they began as a doo-wop group, and they were a polished nightclub act by the time they joined Harvey Fuqua and Gwen Gordy's label Tri-Phi.

In 1963 they switched to Motown but got lost in the crowd. Some members sang background vocals; others served as chauffeurs.

The Spinners did have a hit in 1970, but by then they were ready to leave, which they did one year later.

The name of their hit song said it all: "It's a Shame."

(Left) The 1962 Spinners: From left: Edgar "Chico" Edwards, Bobbie Smith, Henry Fambrough, Billy Henderson, Pervis Jackson. (Right) Though the Originals worked primarily as a quartet – whose members included, from left, Walter Gaines, Crathman Spencer, Henry Dixon, and former mail carrier Freddie Gorman – the original fifth member, shown here at right, was former Contour Joe Stubbs, brother of Levi. (Below) Saundra Mallett and the other Elgins: Cleo Miller, Robert Fleming, Johnny Dawson.

GLADYS KNIGHT
&
THE PIPS

WHEN Gladys Knight
and the Pips signed with
Motown in 1966, they joined an
awesome constellation of stars.
But it was the stars who were
intimidated.

Otis Williams of the
Temptations remembered
sharing a stage with the group
in Cleveland in the early sixties
and seeing the Pips hit the
stage dancing. "They were
unstoppable," he said. "To be
honest, they chewed up our
butts but good. . . . I said,
'Fellas, we gotta go back to
Detroit and do some more
rehearsing!'"

Gladys Knight and the
Pips seemed a natural Motown
act. First, they were family:
Gladys, brother Merald
("Bubba"), and cousins
Edward Patten and William
Guest. Second, they were
already polished artists after
a decade of nightclub appearances, having trained for years
with Cholly Atkins and
Maurice King – all of this long
before those two giants joined
Motown. Finally, they shared
Gordy's crossover dream of
playing the best clubs all over
the world.

Gladys Knight and the Pips, who formed in 1952 and whose first professional job, in 1956, was at a YWCA tea, haven't changed one Pip since the early years. They are (above) Gladys, William "Cousin Red" Guest, Edward "Cousin Ed" Patten, and brother Merald "Bubba" Knight. (Left) At the Watts Summer Festival in the late sixties.

When the group
opened at New York's
Waldorf-Astoria in 1973, Bubba
was exuberant. "Man," he
said, "we've been rehearsing
for this show for twenty-one
years. Life has been one long
rehearsal."

The rehearsal had
begun in 1952, when seven-
year-old Gladys, along with
Bubba, their sister, and two
cousins, provided entertainment for Bubba's backyard
birthday party.

By 1957 the Pips – a
name they got from another
cousin's nickname – had begun
to work the clubs. In 1961 they
had a hit record, "Every Beat
of My Heart." A year after
signing with Motown, in 1967,
they hit the top of the charts
with a driven version of
"I Heard It through the
Grapevine."

But by 1973 this proud
family group was feeling left
out at Motown and chose to
move on. They left with a
Number Two hit: "Neither
One of Us (Wants to Be the
First to Say Goodbye)."

Gladys and the Pips at a Detroit factory in 1966. "We struck a groove right away," Motown session bandleader Earl Van Dyke remembered. "We knew how Gladys sang. . . . Gladys had a drive just like we had, and the more you drive Gladys, the more she sings." After "Grapevine" in 1967, the group scored with "The End of Our Road," "The Nitty Gritty," "Friendship Train" (right) – featuring some classic choo-choo moves by the Pips – and "If I Were Your Woman," a hit in 1970. By then the group were regulars in the best showcase rooms around the country.

You're like a diamond, but she treats you like glass.

Yet you beg her to love you, but me you don't ask.

If I were your w o m a n ,

If I were your w o m a n

If I were your w o m a n ,

If I were your w o m a n

If I were your w o m a n ,

If I were your w o m a n

here's what I'd do:

what would you do

what would you do

*I'd **never**,*

no, no,

stop loving you.

If I Were Your Woman
By Gloria Jones, Pam
Sawyer and Clay
McMurray

FOUR TOPS

ONE of the most popular songs around Hitsville was a corny company tune written by Smokey Robinson. When Gordy got the staff together to sing the lyrics – "Nowhere will you find more unity than at Hitsville, USA" – they sang it like they meant it. The Four Tops had a schmaltzy tune of their own, all about having fun and trying to touch the sun: "Every boy and girl around the world knows there will always be through eternity . . . the four of us." And when the four of them sang it, they sang it like they meant it, too.

The Four Tops have entered their fourth decade without any personnel changes. It's always been Levi Stubbs, Abdul "Duke" Fakir, Lawrence Payton, and Obie Benson. And they've always been pros.

They came from Detroit's blue-collar North End. Fakir recalls: "It was hard working, and all the kids were very competitive. They were either into sports or there were groups singing on every corner.

"Obie, Levi, and Lawrence – we all played ball. In the evening we put our

Sugar pie honey bunch

you know that I'm *weak* for you.

Can't help myself, I love you and nobody else.

I Can't Help Myself
By Brian Holland,
Lamont Dozier and
Eddie Holland

(Left) The Four Tops, originally called the Four Aims, have worked together since 1954. They are, from left, Levi Stubbs, Renaldo "Obie" Benson, Abdul "Duke" Fakir, and Lawrence Payton. (Above and right) The Tops cruise the Hitsville, USA neighborhood.

I really want you

Another day,

mm mmm

'nother night,

I really want you

I l o n g to hold you tight,

mm mmm

'cause I'm so alone.

Baby, I n e e d your lovin',

got

to have all your lovin'.

Baby, I n e e d your lovin',

got

to have all your lovin'.

Baby I Need Your Loving
By Brian Holland,
Lamont Dozier and
Eddie Holland

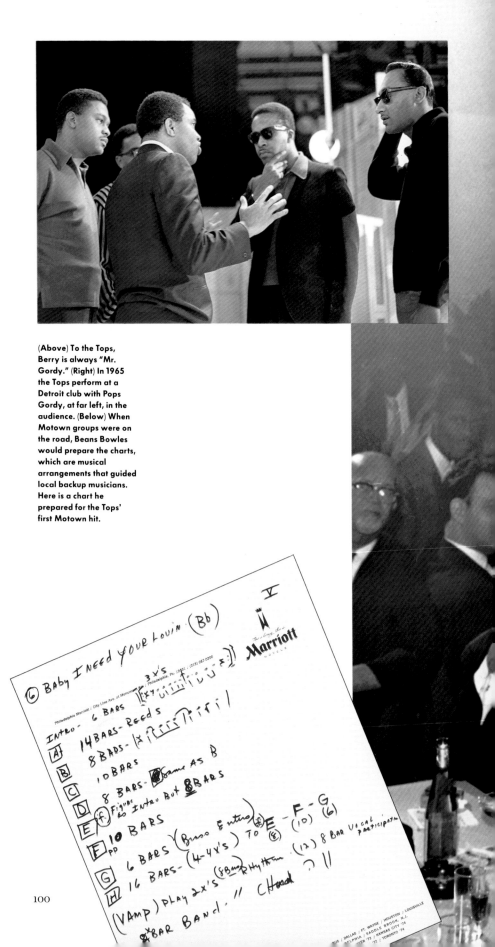

(Above) To the Tops, Berry is always "Mr. Gordy." (Right) In 1965 the Tops perform at a Detroit club with Pops Gordy, at far left, in the audience. (Below) When Motown groups were on the road, Beans Bowles would prepare the charts, which are musical arrangements that guided local backup musicians. Here is a chart he prepared for the Tops' first Motown hit.

100

voices together, and there it
was: We knew it the moment
we hit our first note."

The guys worked for
whoever would hire them, and
they worked hard to please
their varied audiences. At local
clubs they could sing jazz, but if
they had dates in Miami or the
Catskills, they could sing "O
Sole Mio" and "My Yiddische
Mama." In Montreal they
could sing in French.

Joining Motown in
1963, the Tops had a long string
of hits, among them "Baby I
Need Your Loving," "I Can't
Help Myself," "Reach Out
I'll Be There," "Standing in
the Shadows of Love," and
"Bernadette."

For all their years on-
stage, the Tops were not great
movers – and they knew it.
They avoided Cholly Atkins's
dance classes. As Fakir
recalled, "It came down to:
What do you want me to do,
sing or dance? We chose to
concentrate on singing."

Most of the time the
Tops let their singing do the
dancing. That was just fine.
The simplicity of their moves
freed Payton, Fakir, and

darl i n g

reach o u t

come on girl,
reach out for me

reach o u t

reach out for me.

I'll be t h e r e
with a love
that will shelter y o u.

Reach Out I'll Be There
By Brian Holland,
Lamont Dozier and
Eddie Holland

Levi Stubbs was one
of the most emphatic
singers ever to grace the
Motown label. When
Gordy first signed the
group, he had them
record for his Workshop
Jazz label. They were
soon switched to the
Motown label, where
they began turning
Holland-Dozier-Holland
songs into classics.

Benson to wail behind Stubbs,
to express an unabashed joy in
performing, to revel in each
other's company.

The Tops never lost
their perspective. When critics
raved about Stubbs's booming
voice, he'd shrug. "It was just a
natural thing," he said. "I don't
consider myself as being a heck
of a singer." Instead Stubbs
credited the Tops' successes
to writer/producers Holland,
Dozier, and Holland: "Because
of them, the Four Tops were
the Four Tops." In fact, shortly
after H-D-H left Motown in
1968, the Tops began to drift.
"Without them, we couldn't get
a hit," said Payton.

There was something
else. "As Motown grew . . .
they couldn't concentrate on
everybody. They got *so* big.
And so we just had to leave."

"Motown Mondays" at the Roostertail nightclub in Detroit meant that anyone might pop on-stage for the finale. This night in 1966, it's the Tops with Phil Everly, Marvin Gaye, Don Everly, Diana Ross (partly obscured), and Mary Wilson.

The
MOTOWN
ALBUM

W

HEN Berry Gordy talked about crossing over, he didn't just mean record charts and racial barriers. He was talking about oceans.

The push for international exposure and sales began in 1963, when Motown was just becoming successful. Esther Gordy Edwards, Berry's sister and a Motown senior vice president, and Barney Ales, the company's vice president for sales, led the charge, traveling to England, Belgium, Germany, and the Netherlands to try to set up distribution and promotion deals.

The British, busy mapping out their invasion of the American pop scene, were friendly. After all, the Beatles and Rolling Stones both had credited the Motown Sound as an important influence. Still, Motown secured only a few European distribution deals. And many promoters were wary of booking a Motown Revue without a major, recognizable star.

Help came from pirate radio. Broadcasting from ships cruising off the British coastline, unlicensed stations such

L o v e is here

Love is here

and oh my darling, now you're gone.

now you're gone

L o v e is here

Love is here

and oh my darling, now you're gone.

now you're gone

**Love Is Here and
Now You're Gone**
By Brian Holland,
Lamont Dozier and
Eddie Holland

The American Invasion hit Britain in 1965, when Motown established a London-based label, Tamla-Motown, and celebrated with tours. (Left) The visitors range from Berry's young son Terry to Pops Gordy. (Right) In London they were a hit, though one wire service called the revue "pop groups from the Motown company of Chicago." In the front row, from left: Florence Ballard, Mary Wilson, Diana Ross, Betty Kelley, Rosalyn Ashford, Martha Reeves. In the back row: David Ruffin, Melvin Franklin, Smokey Robinson, Otis Williams, Bobby Rogers, Paul Williams, Eddie Kendricks, Ronnie White, Pete Moore.

STOP! *In the name of l o v e*
before you break my h e a r t.

STOP! *In the name of l o v e ,*
before you break my h e a r t.

as Radio Caroline beamed the Motown Sound into London. Soon, the government-controlled BBC found itself playing catch-up when the Supremes' "Baby Love" hit Number One on the British charts.

In 1965 Motown set up Tamla-Motown Records in London and sent the Motown Revue on a twenty-one-show tour of the U.K. Mary Wilson remembered it as "the infamous Ghost Tour" because of photos of the group which appeared in a newspaper there: "Apparently, the photographer hadn't taken too many photos of blacks, and the lighting was all wrong." The paper made matters worse by highlighting the performers' faces with grease pencils. "Honey, I know I'm black, but this is ridiculous," declared Florence Ballard.

But to British audiences, the Supremes looked just fine. One critic called their music "more sophisticated, more professional than the British brand. The punch of the big beat in a velvet glove."

Think it over.

Stop! In the Name of Love
By Brian Holland,
Lamont Dozier and
Eddie Holland

(Left) Flo, Mary, and Diana at Piccadilly Circus. (Right) Charm school pays off. In late 1968 the Supremes, with new member Cindy Birdsong at right, meet the Queen Mother after a royal command performance at the London Palladium. Years later (below), it's the Jackson 5's turn. Father Joe Jackson leads the boys down the line as Elton John watches.

(Right) The Jackson 5 play tourist in Japan. On a tour of the Far East in the fall of 1966 (above right), the Supremes performed in Tokyo, Okinawa, Taiwan, Hong Kong, and Manila. At the naval base in Yokosuka, they played for four thousand men on the U.S.S. *Coral Sea.* In Tokyo a group of geishas imitates the Supremes' famous "stop" move for "Stop! In the Name of Love." Berry Gordy imitates Cholly Atkins.

The Four Tops in England
and the Supremes in
France. In late 1965 the
Supremes played the
Olympia Music Hall in
Paris with the Miracles
and Martha and the
Vandellas. In the
audience were two great
singers: Sarah Vaughan
and Marlene Dietrich.

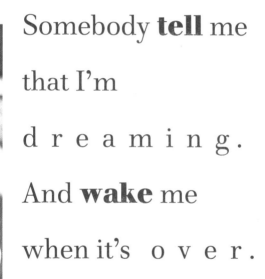

(Above) The Tops sign a few in Paris in 1966. (Right) The Vandellas out on London town. From left: Betty, Rosalyn, Martha.

Somebody **shake** m e,

wake m e

when it's o v e r.

Somebody **tell** me

that I'm

d r e a m i n g.

And **wake** me

when it's o v e r.

**Shake Me, Wake Me
(When It's Over)**
By Eddie Holland,
Lamont Dozier and
Brian Holland

Oh yes, there were the songs, supplied early on by Smokey Robinson: "The Way You Do the Things You Do," "Get Ready," and "My Girl," with that heartthrob of a bass intro.

And there were the voices: the rugged pleadings of David Ruffin; the perfect falsetto of high tenor Eddie Kendricks; the doo-wopper bass of Melvin Franklin; the solid harmonies of baritone Paul Williams and baritone/second tenor Otis Williams.

But most of all, there were the moves – the classic glides, spins, and dips, the hand movements that, like a soul hula, helped embellish the story line of each song. All accomplished, of course, with precision and harmony, like a crack drill team from R&B heaven.

Lean and handsome, smooth and suave, impeccably and uniformly dressed in sharp suits and ties or shimmering tuxes, they were, indeed, the Temptin' Temptations, and they were like no other group ever to perform on Motown Records.

The Temptations were not primarily a dance act, but sometimes it'd be hard to convince audiences, especially the ones at the after-school bandstand shows, where kids in the bleachers would sway together from side to side, forward and backward, matching the Tempts' hand movements.

Next to the Supremes
the Tempts had the most hits
of any group on the label –
thirty-five Top Forty hits in an
eleven-year span starting in
1964. And, despite the loss of
three of their original five
members and a dramatic
change in their sound, they
never broke stride.

The Temptations
were melded together from
two Detroit groups, the Primes
(from which came Kendricks
and Paul Williams) and the
Distants (Franklin and Otis
Williams). After replacing
their original fifth member
with singer/drummer Ruffin,
the Primes signed with
Motown in 1961. Their new
name was Gordy's idea.

The Temptations
were an instant hit in concert
but not with their first records,
until they hooked up with
Smokey Robinson. Inspired by
the thousand-dollar bonuses
Gordy handed out to writers of
Number One songs, he came
up with "The Way You Do the
Things You Do" in 1964, on a
drive with fellow Miracle Bobby
Rogers. The song peaked at
Number Eleven – a hit position

(Left) The Tantalizin' Tempts in 1967. For young audiences the guys went tieless but still could look snappy in tuxedos complete with cummerbunds. The four-headed microphone was David Ruffin's invention. The Tempts, obviously anxious to please their record company, wore any colors they were asked to. Any colors.

Throughout their years at Motown, Cholly Atkins helped the Temptations to polish their act, but Melvin Franklin credited Paul Williams with giving the group its first steps. "I think he's the best dancer I ever worked with," he said. Williams learned some of his best moves from an old hoofer named Peg Leg Bates – who actually had a wooden leg. From left: Eddie Kendricks, Melvin Franklin, Paul Williams, Otis Williams, and David Ruffin practiced two hours every day at the Artists Development Studio.

for the Temptations, but no bonus for Robinson. That would come a year later with "My Girl," on which Robinson had Ruffin sing lead, figuring his rougher voice might "counterbalance" the sweet love song. Smokey got his bonus.

The Tempts had several more hits with Robinson, including "It's Growing" and "My Baby," which established Ruffin as the group's primary lead singer, and "Get Ready," on which Kendricks rode his true falsetto over the driving beat. Again the idea was counterbalance; again it worked.

At the first sign of a slowdown – "Get Ready" only reached Number Twenty-Nine – Gordy pulled a switch of producers. "Get Ready" had beaten out "Ain't Too Proud to Beg," produced by Norman Whitfield, at a Quality Control meeting. Now, Motown released it, and when it hit Number Thirteen, Whitfield took over the Tempts.

He and writing partner Eddie Holland followed "Ain't Too Proud" with "Beauty Is Only Skin Deep" and "(I

Hats off, the Temptations cut a record at Hitsville's Studio A in 1967. Otis recalled the group's uncertainty about producer Norman Whitfield's idea of adding sound effects to "I Wish It Would Rain," but the Tempts let Whitfield have his way, and they wound up with a Number One R&B hit.

So twiddle-dee-dee twiddle-dee-dum

Look out baby   'cause here I come.

Know) I'm Losing You," both Top Ten records.

Whitfield soon would take the Temptations – and the Motown Sound – in a new direction. But within the group there were already profound changes.

Paul Williams, once a lead singer who'd been the architect of the Tempts' style and the choreographer of all their early dance moves, including the famed "Temptation Walk," had faded into the background. Beset by personal problems, he began drinking heavily and using drugs.

Meanwhile Ruffin began to make demands for star billing and more money that set him apart from the rest of the group. He had already taken to traveling to concerts in a separate limo. In mid-1968, when he missed a performance so that he could see a girl-friend's nightclub perfor-mance, he and the group part-ed company. The Temptations' first golden era was over.

By the time Marvin Gaye had begun to ask "What's going on?" in the early seven-ties, the Temptations had been

turning social issues into song for several years.

More than any other group, they symbolized Motown at a crossroad. They had reached such show biz pinnacles as the Copacabana Club and the "Ed Sullivan Show." They could tux it up or throw it down, stand straight up and deliver "Old Man River" or Temptation Walk all over "Ain't Too Proud to Beg."

But in the late sixties – which is when the sixties really began – that was all wrong. When what the popular press called the Youthquake hit, you fell on one side or the other of the new fault line. Yes or No. Black or White. Us or Them. The solution or the problem.

Norman Whitfield had the solution. He'd been listening to the work of such upstarts as Sly Stone, who was mixing R&B with rock and roll and the sentiments of the times, and Whitfield thought the Tempts ought to get in on the action.

The immediate result: "Cloud Nine," featuring Ruffin's replacement, Dennis Edwards. The song, which

And I'm bringing you a love that's true,

so get *ready*   so get *r e a d y.*

Get Ready
By William "Smokey"
Robinson

In 1967 the Temptations
glided into the Copa –
and into the mainstream.
"Success there was crucial
for us," said Otis Williams,
"since it symbolized
acceptance by the
entertainment business
at large." Melvin tickles
the ivories at a Copa
rehearsal while Otis
Williams confers with
Harvey Fuqua and
Cholly Atkins.

I've got sun s h i n e

on a c l o u d y day.

When it's cold outside,

I've got

the month of May.

I guess you say,

what can make me

feel this way?

My girl,
my girl my girl
talking 'bout my g i r l.
my girl

My Girl
By William "Smokey"
Robinson and Ronald
White

many thought was about drugs ("You're a million miles from reality"), broke new ground. So did "War" and "Ball of Confusion (That's What the World Is Today)," with its references to segregation, unemployment, taxes, birth control, drug abuse, the draft, riots, Indians, and even the Beatles.

The music, like Sly Stone's, was multilayered, sputtering, electronic, experimental. Dennis Edwards, who came from the Contours, was gruff and explosive, expressive in a way no Temptation had been before.

Onstage and on album covers, it was off with the tuxes, on with the leather jackets, the capes, the paisley scarves.

The new sound reached an even larger audience and clearly influenced numerous other musicians and record producers, black and white.

Not everyone, of course, was happy with the changes. After "Ball of Confusion," the group hit with the wistful "Just My Imagination

In December 1968 the Temptations join with the Supremes for an album and an NBC special. "It's so much fun working with the boy groups," Diana Ross said, "because you kind of put them uptight and they put you uptight. It was like a challenge. Everybody's trying to outdo you, so we came up with some great material."

The way you smell so *sweet,*
The way you smell so sweet

(Running Away with Me)," written by Whitfield with Barrett Strong. The song "was basically forced on us," Kendricks complained. "The public said they didn't want us doing psychedelic music."

While the Temptations worked their balancing act with the public, more changes were taking place inside the group. Paul Williams's health continued to decline, and in 1971 he left the group. Two years later he committed suicide just blocks from Motown's original home.

In 1971 Kendricks, a close friend of Paul, also departed, expressing unhappiness with the group and with Motown. He stayed with the company, however, enjoying success with "Keep on Truckin'" and "Boogie Down."

Richard Street, who had worked at Motown after his time with the Distants, replaced Paul, and Damon Harris of the Tempos, a Temptations clone act, came in for Kendricks.

A year later the new group scored a Number One hit with "Papa Was a Rollin'

Stone." Since then the lineup has changed seven times. The Tempts carry on, with Otis Williams, Franklin, and Street anchoring the group.

In 1982 Ruffin and Kendricks returned for a reunion tour and album. In 1983 the entire cast of *The Big Chill* sang the Temptations' "Ain't Too Proud to Beg." In 1985 Hall and Oates joined with Ruffin and Kendricks for a concert and a hit record. And in 1989 the group did the Temptations Walk into the Rock and Roll Hall of Fame.

They were not the Tempts of Hitsville, USA on West Grand, but to Otis Williams, there were, and are, no voids.

"The Temptations still stand today," he said, "not in spite of those who left us but because of them."

you know you could've been
 some p e r f u m e .

W e l l ,
you could've been anything
 that you
 wanted to
and I can t e l l

 the way you do
 the things you do.

*The way you do
the things you do*

Ah b a b y

*The way you do
the things you do*

**The Way You Do the
Things You Do**
By William "Smokey"
Robinson and Bobby
Rogers

Long after they left the
Temptations, Eddie
Kendricks, at left, and
David Ruffin remained
friends, working together
on the road and teaming
up with admirers Hall and
Oates for a television
appearance and
successful single, a
medley of "The Way You
Do the Things You Do"
and "My Girl." Although
a reunion with the Tempts
didn't mend all the
breaks, Otis said of them:
"They will always be
Temptations."

*I*n the early sixties pop music – especially rock and roll – was not welcome on prime-time television.

To most network executives, teen music was not only unlistenable; it had been scientifically proven to lead directly to delinquency.

Dick Clark of "American Bandstand" was among the first to host rock and roll and rhythm and blues acts. But he was on in the afternoons, as were local bandstand shows.

By 1965 rock and R&B – and the youth market that supported them – had gotten too big for prime time to ignore. ABC and NBC put "Shindig" and "Hullabaloo" on the air, and Motown stars appeared regularly.

But the big prime-time variety shows hadn't advanced far beyond the days of Ed Sullivan censoring Elvis Presley's hips and Steve Allen giving him a hound dog as a prop. Television executives continued to limit shows to the biggest names – say, the Beatles – or to middle-of-the-road acts that would blend in with magicians and comics.

By the time the Supremes appeared on "Top of the Pops" in the fall of 1965, they were veterans in front of the camera, having appeared on the "Ed Sullivan Show" the winter before as well as on the Dean Martin, Jackie Gleason, and Steve Allen variety shows.

Dick Clark and Ed Sullivan were early and enthusiastic supporters of Motown on television. The notoriously stiff Sullivan loosened up with the Jackson 5, Gladys Knight and the Pips, and Smokey Robinson.

England loved Motown, and so did English television. In 1965 the show "Ready, Steady, Go" devoted its hour to Motown. On the show, which was hosted by Dusty Springfield, the Four Tops (at left) appeared with Martha and the Vandellas, the Miracles, the Supremes, Marvin Gaye, the Temptations, and Mary Wells.

Motown, which was grooming its artists to cross show-business barriers, had no trouble giving the programs just what they wanted: clean-cut, elegantly dressed performers dancing and singing love songs. The perfect example, of course, was the Supremes.

At first, Motown acts were not exactly household names, as Ed Sullivan's introductory remarks for the Miracles clearly showed: "Ladies and gentlemen, let's have a warm welcome for a great group of guys from Detroit, Michigan . . . Smokey – and the Little Smokeys!"

But by 1968 the Supremes and the Temptations, who would have a hit record together with "I'm Gonna Make You Love Me," had teamed up for an NBC special, "TCB – Taking Care of Business: Diana Ross and the Supremes with the Temptations." It was a landmark. As one critic noted, "It was the first major black television special in history."

The first presentation from Motown's television/theatrical division was "Diana," televised on Sunday, April 18, 1971. Gordy, with Suzanne de Passe and producer George Schlatter among others, worked on the spectacular, which included guest stars Bill Cosby, Danny Thomas, and the Jackson 5. One memorable number had Michael Jackson dressed up like Frank Sinatra, singing "It Was a Very Good Year" with some slightly altered lyrics: "When I was two years old/I was four years old."

Motown's first two television productions featured their biggest groups, the Supremes and the Temptations, together. In December 1968 it was "TCB [Taking Care of Business]"; the next November, "GIT [Get it Together] on Broadway." Diana Ross got the star's role, but all the Supremes and Tempts got plenty of chances to dress up, perform skits, and sing songs that had nothing to do with the Motown Sound.

ORGET "black." The Supremes were the biggest female pop group ever. As calculated by *Billboard* magazine's record popularity charts, they ranked as the third biggest pop act of the sixties, trailing only the Beatles and Elvis. They were America's answer to the Beatles and the entire British Invasion. After twelve Number One hits, they were beyond a sound. They were a symbol of what could happen to three girls from a poor neighborhood in Detroit.

Berry Gordy's wildest crossover dreams had come true; the Supremes were the perfect vehicle for Motown's ride into the mainstream, to Las Vegas, to the Copacabana, to the network variety shows.

But it took patience, it took grooming, and it took a relationship between mentor and star that put stresses on the group even as it soared.

The girls were, first of all, high school friends from the Brewster Housing Projects in Detroit; they formed the Primettes as a sister group to the Primes. Originally, there were four members: Betty

Before they were the Supremes, they were the Primettes. From left: Barbara Martin, Mary Wilson, Florence Ballard; Miss Ross, already on top, completed the lineup in 1961. Martin replaced Betty McGlown, who was in the group when it formed in 1959 but left to get married. After signing with Motown, Martin left to have a baby, and the Supremes decided to make do as a trio. As Diana told Flo and Mary: "If the three of us can't make it, then we won't make it." But they did, and in 1965 they played the Copa for the first time.

McGlown (later replaced by Barbara Martin), Florence Ballard, Mary Wilson, and Diane Ross (who changed her name to Diana later). As a young girl hanging around the neighborhood watching the formative Miracles rehearse, Ross had met Smokey Robinson. Through Smokey the Primettes got a Motown audition. The story goes that Gordy told them he wouldn't consider signing them until they'd finished school.

Having seen the inside of Hitsville, the girls were hooked. Every day after school, they hung out at the studios until they became known as "the girls."

"We were just *court-ing* Motown," Ross recalls, "making pests of ourselves."

The girls' drive to succeed was obvious. Ross held a job in a department store, went to modeling school, and worked as a secretary at Motown for Berry Gordy.

If the Primettes had had no talent to back up their charm and energy, they wouldn't have been welcome at Hitsville. But they could

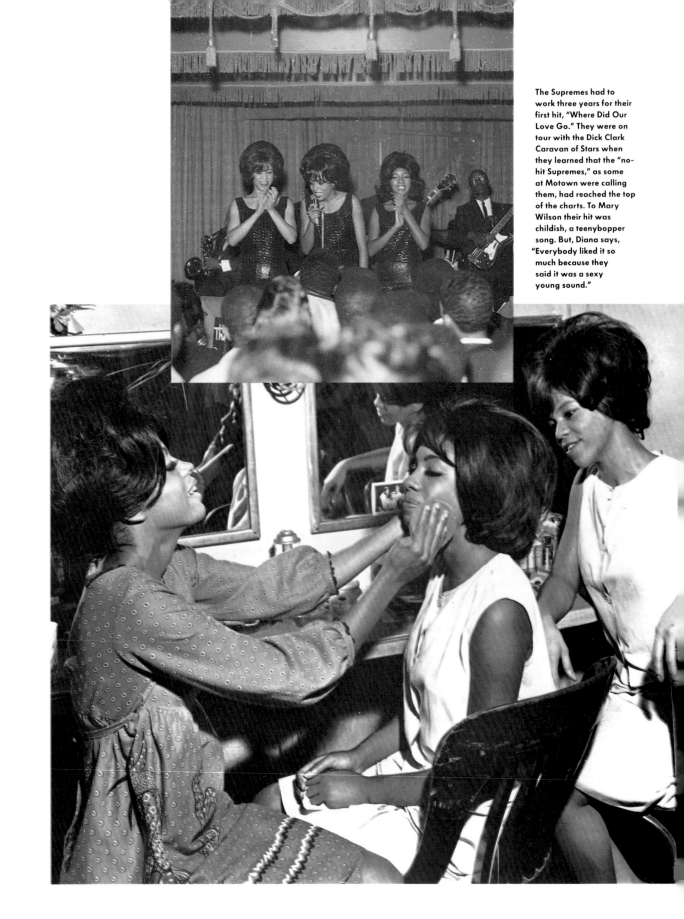

The Supremes had to work three years for their first hit, "Where Did Our Love Go." They were on tour with the Dick Clark Caravan of Stars when they learned that the "no-hit Supremes," as some at Motown were calling them, had reached the top of the charts. To Mary Wilson their hit was childish, a teenybopper song. But, Diana says, "Everybody liked it so much because they said it was a sexy young sound."

Baby, baby, where did our love go?

Ooh, don't you want me?

baby, baby

Don't you want me no more?

baby, baby

Ooh, baby.

Where Did Our Love Go
By Brian Holland,
Lamont Dozier and
Eddie Holland

After their first big hit, said Mary, " We were local heroes. Wherever we went in our neighborhoods, people would call out to us and wave. In the projects 'Where Did Our Love Go' could be heard coming out of every window."

sing. It's true that Ross, whom Gordy picked to be lead singer, had a thin voice, but it was distinctive. As a performer she was clearly the most engaging, with her big eyes and bigger smile.

Gordy signed the girls in 1961, but not as the Primettes. He asked for a new name, and Hitsville employees, from secretaries to stars, chipped in ideas. It was Flo who picked the Supremes.

The Supremes became a trio after Barbara Martin left, and they began at the bottom, singing backup vocals and serving as an opening act on the Motortown Revues.

But they felt lost, Mary recalled. "There were already so many girl groups, and we did not really fit because we were not soulful and we didn't get down as much as we wanted to."

Gordy felt that Ross's unique voice would set the group apart, but their first six records, all flops, didn't seem to prove him out. Then he suggested that the girls begin working with Eddie and Brian Holland and Lamont Dozier. One of their first recordings,

But mama said,

You can't hurry love,

n o you just have to wait,

she said,

love don't come e a s y ,

it's a game of give and take.

You Can't Hurry Love
By Eddie Holland,
Lamont Dozier and
Brian Holland

The Supremes party
at Loucye Gordy
Wakefield's home in
1964. (Right) That same
year, the girls visit
Northwestern High
School. Most kids in
the Brewster Projects
neighborhood attended
Northwestern, but Diana
went to Cass Technical,
where the academic
standards were higher.
There, she is still
remembered by teachers
as "Diane, that girl who
said she'd be a star."

"Where Did Our Love Go," hit the top of the charts in 1964. The Supremes followed up with four more Holland-Dozier-Holland Number One hits: "Baby Love," "Come See about Me," "Stop! In the Name of Love," and "Back in My Arms Again."

The softer, less soulful sound that had worried Wilson turned out to be the key to the Supremes' success.

But behind the scenes, trouble was brewing.

By 1965 Gordy, who had made the Supremes his top priority at Motown, had formed a closer personal relationship with Ross that caused some jealousy. His decision to move Ross increasingly to the front of the group came at the expense of Ballard and Wilson.

Ballard, clearly unhappy about being a backup singer, began missing shows due to "illness." In the fall of 1967 the group became Diana Ross and the Supremes, and within the year Gordy replaced Ballard with Cindy Birdsong.

In November 1969 Motown announced that Diana Ross would pursue a solo

"The dreams we had shared for so many years were finally coming true now – overnight," Wilson remembered. But even as the Supremes drew backstage mobs wherever they played, Ballard, sitting between Diana and Mary, found that success was not bringing her happiness.

why don't cha b a b y .

Let me *be* why don't cha b a b y

'cause you don't really love me

you just keep me *h a n g i n '* on.

You Keep Me Hanging On
By Eddie Holland,
Lamont Dozier and
Brian Holland

career. Her final performance as a Supreme took place in January 1970 in Las Vegas, where the group sang what had become the signature tune of her departure: "Someday We'll Be Together."

Ironically, the song was recorded with neither Wilson nor Birdsong singing backup, but with regular session vocalists.

Selecting seasoned performer Jean Terrell to take Ross's spot, the Supremes had several more hits and personnel changes before disbanding in 1977.

There was one reunion. In February 1976, Ross and Wilson attended the funeral of Flo Ballard, who had died of a heart attack at age thirty-two. As the crowd filed out of the funeral home, the organist played "Someday We'll Be Together."

That day finally came in January 1988, when the Supremes were inducted into the Rock and Roll Hall of Fame.

Backstage and onstage at the Venetian Room of the Fairmont Hotel in San Francisco. The Supremes made no effort to hide the distance that had grown between them, but onstage they continued to mesh in performance, as if they were strutting their stuff for the first time. "We were still wearing our million-dollar smiles," said Mary, "but Flo and I were crying inside."

I wanna say, I wanna say, I wanna s a y

Some d a y

we'll be together.

Yes we will, yes we will.

Say some d a y

we'll be together.

Someday We'll Be Together
By Jackey Beavers,
Johnny Bristol and
Harvey Fuqua

In the spring of 1967 Flo was replaced by Cindy Birdsong, who had been rehearsed and groomed for weeks. Birdsong fit right in when she made her debut at the Hollywood Bowl. But Ross was growing away from the group, now billed as Diana Ross and the Supremes. (Right) The group performed on the "Ed Sullivan Show" in late 1967, with Birdsong on the right.

*R*oss left the Supremes, she has said, because she wanted to try a movie career.

Once again, she was in sync with Berry Gordy. Well before Motown moved to Los Angeles, Gordy had been thinking about moving into television and films. By the time he got to Hollywood, he already had a film idea.

A year before he founded Motown, Gordy had met the great jazz singer Billie Holiday. In Diana Ross he felt he had the right star to bring Holiday's personality to a film he entitled *Lady Sings the Blues*.

Ross, however, wasn't certain about taking the part; she was wary, she said, of becoming too closely identified with Lady Day and her music. Once committed, though, she found a way to play the role while remaining true to herself.

"I knew that I could not try to imitate Billie Holiday; she was too special," she said. "What I had to do was try some way inside of me to know her, and maybe that would come through."

To bring jazz singer Billie Holiday's story to the screen, Berry Gordy dug into his own pockets to help finance the $3.6 million film, screened every foot of it, and involved himself in every phase of its production, from rehearsals to soundtrack. (Above) Gordy works with director Michel Legrand.

Critics applauded both Ross's singing and her acting; she won a Golden Globe Award and was nominated for an Academy Award for best actress. The film also earned Oscar nominations for best score and best script. Among the writers was Suzanne de Passe, who rose from road manager and adviser to the Jackson 5 to vice president of Motown in 1972 and then to her current position as president of Motown Productions.

Motown went on to produce *Mahogany* (starring Ross and Billy Dee Williams), *The Bingo Long Traveling All-Stars and Motor Kings*, and, in 1978, *The Wiz*, with Diana as Dorothy and Michael Jackson, in his film debut, as the Scarecrow. None of these, however, met with the same critical or box office success as *Lady Sings the Blues*. Motown also invested in the hit Broadway show *Pippin*. The company's television productions included "Scott Joplin: King of Ragtime" (originally intended as a motion picture) and "Lonesome Dove," the acclaimed 1989 miniseries.

Motown followed *Lady Sings the Blues* in 1975 with another vehicle for Diana Ross. In *Mahogany* (left) she played a model and fashion designer in love with a politician (Billy Dee Williams) who told her, "Success is *nothing* without someone you love to share it with." (Right) Ross portrayed Dorothy and Michael Jackson played the Scarecrow in the 1978 film *The Wiz*.

Ross (above) with Motown vice president Michael Roshkind at the Sunset Boulevard offices and (left) with Berry at the fiftieth-anniversary celebration of the Apollo Theatre in 1985. (Right) Ross reaches out and touches.

Ross gets Suzanne de Passe, president of Motown Productions, into the act. De Passe began working for Motown in 1968 as Gordy's creative assistant; during this time she choreographed the Jackson 5's stage routines, urged the signing of the Commodores, and wrote television specials for Diana Ross and the Jackson 5. Nominated for an Academy Award for her work on *Lady Sings the Blues*, she has won Emmys for producing the television specials "Motown 25," "Motown Returns to the Apollo," and "Lonesome Dove." (Right) Ross dresses down and up.

In 1973 Ross and Marvin Gaye, close friends from the early years at Hitsville, finally made an album together that was imaginatively titled *Diana and Marvin*. (Left) At the time Diana was pregnant, and the demanding recording schedule was exhausting. At the control board with songwriters Valerie Simpson and Nick Ashford, manager Shelly Berger, and Gaye, Diana listens to playback. Diana had three children by her first husband, Bob Silberstein: Chudney Lane, Tracee Joy, and Rhonda Suzanne. She had two boys with her present husband, Arne Naess: Ross Arne and Evan. (Right) Sleeping giants of the future. Diana helped launch the Jackson 5.

As the sixties ended, Motown found itself a tempting target in an intensely competitive business where it no longer was the only option for black performers. With the move to Los Angeles, many artists, producers, writers, and musicians began to leave the company. Some wanted to stay in Detroit; others switched labels, seeking more attention or money. For myriad reasons Motown needed an injection of youth and energy. The Jackson 5 had both.

Although they came from Gary, Indiana, the Jacksons were perfect for the Hollywood version of Motown and just right for television.

At a time of acid rock and psychedelic soul, of war protests and black power, Motown could offer a wholesome family group dressed in 'fros and mod duds and singing nonthreatening pop music.

Motown switched back into gear for the Jacksons. Resurrecting Artists Development to polish the boys' public styles onstage and off, the company prepared for a media blitz that would skyrocket

The family that plays together: (Left) An early publicity photo. (Right) The Jacksons sit for an informal portrait. In the back row, from left: Jermaine, Rebbie, Tito, Marlon. In the front row: Joe, Janet, Michael, Katherine, Randy. "I don't want to brag," said Joe Jackson, "but looking at the kids, I think I've done a good job. It was hard, but it sure has paid off."

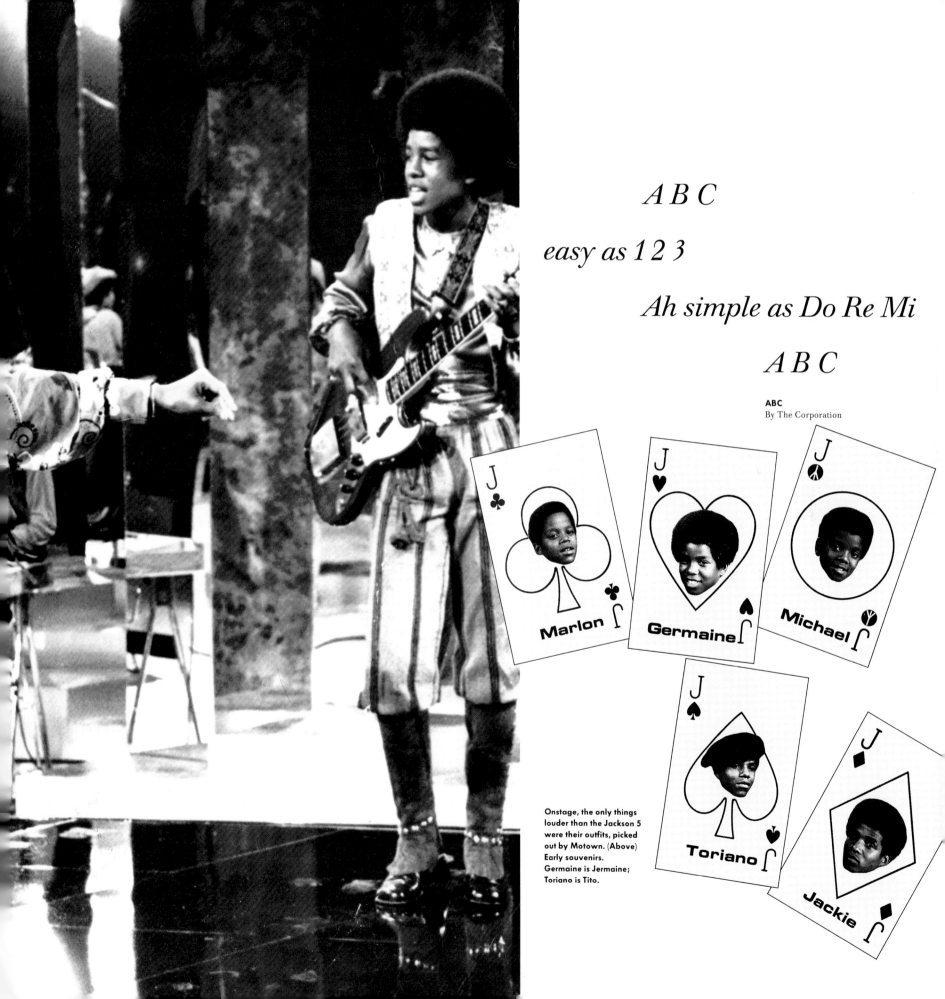

A B C

easy as 1 2 3

Ah simple as Do Re Mi

A B C

ABC
By The Corporation

Onstage, the only things
louder than the Jackson 5
were their outfits, picked
out by Motown. (Above)
Early souvenirs.
Germaine is Jermaine;
Toriano is Tito.

The Jacksons jumped to the top of the charts in 1969 with the first in a series of songs by the Corporation, an umbrella name Gordy came up with for staff writers Freddie Perren, Deke Richards, Fonce Mizell, and himself.

the five young brothers
to stardom.

The Jacksons – from
eleven-year-old Michael to
eighteen-year-old Jackie –
took it all in stride. Already
seasoned performers, their
father had put them through
his own version of Artists
Development.

The older brothers,
Jackie, Tito, and Jermaine,
had learned music by sneaking
off with their father's guitar.
Joe Jackson, who had once
played with an R&B band, the
Falcons, now worked in a Gary
steel mill, but when he discovered his kids' interest in
music, he encouraged them.
He gave instruments to Tito
(guitar) and Jermaine (bass).
Soon, with the six-year-old
Michael playing bongos, doing
perfect James Brown spins,
and singing like an old-time
bluesman, the Jacksons were
winning local talent contests
covering Motown songs such as
the Temptations' "My Girl."

"Those talent shows,"
says Michael, "were our professional education."

With their father act-
ing as teacher and manager,

ROLLING STONE

Why does this eleven year-old stay up past his bedtime?

Michael Jackson—and his six gold records

The Murder of Ruben Salazar
By Hunter S. Thompson

(Left) Suzanne de Passe was the Jackson 5's main woman on the scene. She helped train and dress them and, on the road, served as tour coordinator and general overseer. She remembered seeing the ten-year-old Michael's James Brown imitation. "He had it down to a T – and I had to work to get him away from a lot of it. By spring of 1971 he was on the cover of *Rolling Stone*."

the boys went to Chicago, where they got a full-time gig at a nightclub, sharing the stage with comics and strip-tease acts. Michael remembered his mother, Katherine, worriedly telling Joe: "This is quite a life for a nine-year-old."

The boys won talent shows in Chicago, where they impressed not only the judges but also Bobby Taylor, leader of the Motown group Bobby Taylor and the Vancouvers. Taylor convinced Motown to give the kids an audition.

They passed muster and were invited to a party at Gordy's Detroit mansion, where they were introduced to the rest of Motown. The Jackson 5 stunned the executives and stars with their poise. "They gave us a standing ovation," Michael remembers. "Diana Ross came over at the end and kissed each one of us. She said she loved what she saw and wanted to be part of what we [did]." And when it came time to present the group to the press, it was Diana Ross who did the honors, at a Beverly Hills nightclub.

After a few words of advice from the chairman of the Corporation (far left), the Jackson 5 perform in 1973. "Berry was my teacher and a great one," said Michael; "he told me exactly what he wanted and how he wanted me to help him get it." Michael recalled: "Berry insisted on perfection and attention to detail. I'll never forget his persistence. This was his genius."

Backstage before a show, the Jacksons were relaxed. If they seemed anxious, they were mostly itchy to get onstage. Seconds before the final "Let's go" from the stage manager, Tito might be playing a blues tune on his guitar; Jermaine might be strumming along on his bass. (Left) Michael listens to musician "Wah-Wah" Watson.

Their first single, the supercharged "I Want You Back," came out in 1969 and danced up the charts to Number One. The follow-up, "ABC," moved even faster. The third Number One record was "The Love You Save." The Jackson 5 slowed the musical tempo with "I'll Be There," but it, too, raced to Number One.

Michael was a sensation, not only singing and dancing, but doing a turn as a tiny Frank Sinatra in a Diana Ross TV special.

In their time at Motown, the Jackson 5 had thirteen Top Twenty singles, had a television special and cartoon series built around them, and played a royal command performance for the queen of England.

In 1973 Jermaine married Hazel Gordy, Berry's daughter. When his brothers left Motown in 1975, he stayed, insisting: "I wasn't choosing between families. I was choosing between record companies." He went solo and had hits with "Daddy's Home" and "Let's Get Serious," produced by Stevie Wonder.

December 15, 1973: The marriage of Jermaine Jackson to Hazel Joy Gordy was called a "merging of dynasties" by the press. The wedding, at the Beverly Hills Hotel, had a reported budget of $200,000. The production included 175 doves and 7,000 white camellias. Smokey wrote and sang a wedding song, "From This Time and Place." Among the guests: Coretta Scott King, Diana Ross, Diahann Carroll, Billy Dee Williams, Los Angeles Mayor Tom Bradley and his wife.

I never can say goodbye, g i r l

never can say goodbye

ooh ooh, b a b y

don't wanna let you go girl

I never can say goodbye

no, no, no

no, no, no,

no, no, no

I never can say goodbye girl

Never Can Say Goodbye
By Clifton Davis

Inevitably, the family members went their own ways. While working with his brothers, Michael also ventured out on his own projects, including his role in *The Wiz* and two great albums. The brothers had an emotional reunion with Jermaine on the television special "Motown 25," an anniversary tribute, performing a medley of those early Number One hits. It had been fourteen years since Gordy had sat them down in his house and promised that their first three records would make Number One. "I'm gonna make you the biggest thing in the world, and you're gonna be written about in history books," he had said.

Michael remembered that moment. "We were leaning forward, listening to him, and saying, 'Okay! Okay!'"

Photographic proof (left) that Michael wore white gloves long before "Billie Jean." Michael traced his love of animals to a 1972 world tour, which included a stop in Africa.

LIONEL RICHIE
&
THE COMMODORES

I seemed only right that when the Jackson 5 left Motown, some of the substantial void they created would be filled by the Commodores.

After all, the six-man band from Tuskegee, Alabama, got its start as an opening act for the Jackson 5. At the time – 1971 – the Commodores were unsigned, and it was not an easy job playing hits by the Temptations and Sly and the Family Stone in front of audiences only interested in screaming for the headline act.

Motown rewarded the band with a contract, and the Commodores began paying dividends in 1974, when their first album, *Machine Gun*, became a gold record.

Early on, the group zigzagged from straight-ahead R&B burners to dreamy ballads written by their saxophonist and lead singer, Lionel Richie. "Sweet Love" and "Just to Be Close to You" put the band into the Top Ten twice in 1976. "Easy" kept them there the next year, but so did a funk workout, "Brick House."

The Commodores charged ahead. In 1978 they

The Commodores, one of Motown's best-selling groups, included (left) guitarist Thomas McClary and trumpet player William King. (Right) Saxophonist Lionel Richie and bassist Ronald LaPread. The members met at Alabama's Tuskegee Institute in the late sixties. Walter Orange was the drummer, and Milan Williams played keyboards.

And now that we've come to the end of our rainbow,

there's something I m u s t say out loud.

You're once, twice, three t i m e s a lady,

and I l o v e you.

Three Times a Lady
By Lionel B. Richie, Jr.

The Commodores on a natural high in 1979. As the decade began, they were scrounging for work when, as Lionel recalled, their manager ran into Suzanne de Passe, a childhood friend. "She said, 'I have a problem. I have the Jackson 5 and I'm looking for a front act to go on the road with their first U.S. tour.' [Their manager] said, 'Look no further; they're in my apartment.' That's how the Commodores got launched."

appeared in the disco film
Thank God It's Friday with
Donna Summer. Two more
Lionel-at-the-piano love songs,
"Three Times a Lady" and
"Still," went to Number One.

  With his songs pulling
his group out of the crowded
ranks of R&B funk bands,
Richie began to get the attention of a solo star. But the decision to leave the group was a
hard one; he'd been with the
band since college days. When
he wrote the title tune for the
film *Endless Love* and
performed a duet with Diana
Ross on the soundtrack album,
and even when he began work
on his first solo album in 1981,
he still insisted he'd continue
working with the Commodores.

  The final decision,
however, was mutual. After he
left, Lionel admitted: "I think
the guys maybe wanted me out
more than I even wanted to
leave so that they could have
the opportunity to get some
recognition. Maybe they
thought I was overshadowing
them. Maybe I was."

  Without Richie the
Commodores became strangers
to the charts until 1985. The

Between 1974 and 1980
the Commodores' albums
averaged sales of two
million copies each. Their
first four albums went
gold (500,000 copies
sold), their next two were
certified platinum (one
million sold), and they
followed with a double
platinum and two triple
platinum albums. With
Lionel at the forefront, the
group had nine Top Ten
pop singles. In the video
age, clothes made the
man, and when it came
to making fashion
statements, Lionel
was not exactly shy.

previous year they had added
a new lead singer, J. D.
Nicholas, and had delivered
"Nightshift."

Richie, meantime,
continued to romance audiences with three songs that
added up to one message:
"Truly," "You Are," "My
Love." He upped the beat with
"All Night Long" and his 1983
album, *Can't Slow Down*,
broke Motown records as the
company's best-selling album
ever, at fourteen million
copies. Richie also wrote
"Missing You" for Diana Ross,
produced a hit album for
Kenny Rogers, performed at
the 1984 summer Olympics'
closing ceremonies, and wrote
"We Are the World" with
Michael Jackson.

Early in his career
Richie professed to be awe-
struck whenever he ran into
other Motown artists: "I
approach them like legends."
In fact, his singing and songwriting can stand with the best
of Robinson, Wonder, Gaye,
and Michael Jackson. He has
simply joined the ranks.

Behind the scenes:
(Above) William King and
Lionel flank Motown
publicity director Bob
Jones. (Left) Lionel with
former Motown president
Jay Lasker, at left, and
Miller London, the
vice president of sales
and marketing. (Right)
Lionel, who co-wrote
"We Are the World," is
sandwiched by producer
Quincy Jones, at left,
and artists manager
Ken Kragen, who
spearheaded the USA
for Africa production.

War, hunhhh! yeah.

s the seventies began,
Americans were increasingly
turning against the war in
Vietnam. At Motown, Norman
Whitfield and Barrett Strong
came up with "War," the
perfect song to reflect this
dissension.

The Temptations
originally cut the song on their
Psychedelic Shack album, but
when it came time to issue a
single, Motown backed off. A
single, after all, represented
a statement the group – and the
company – was willing to make
on Top Forty radio, where the
message could be repeated
endlessly.

Although the Tempts
had been singing "message"
songs such as "Cloud Nine"
and "Ball of Confusion" for
some time, they were still
Motown's elite, and "War"
was simply too controversial
for them.

Motown drafted
Edwin Starr to record the song.
Starr – real name Charles
Hatcher – was a veteran singer
and writer who'd had hits
before joining Motown, includ-
ing "Stop Her on Sight" and
"Agent Double-O-Soul," a

B 454L

GUESS WHO'S COMING HOME
Black Fighting Men Recorded Live in Vietnam

Motown addressed the
issue of the Vietnam War
on a rare spoken-word
album released by its
Black Forum subsidiary
in 1970.

What i s it good for?

Absolutely nothing.

Edwin Starr, who switched from secret agent man to antiwar protester in 1970 with Norman Whitfield and Barrett Strong's "War." A follow-up, "Stop the War Now," failed. "We just about wore that message out with the first record," said Starr. Rare Earth Records signed progressive rock acts geared to FM's emerging album-rock format. Among the heavier bands: Stoney and Meatloaf (below).

sendup of James Bond. On Gordy Records he had a Top Ten hit with his own composition, the foot-stomping "Twenty-Five Miles." And then came "War," which Starr took to Number One.

"The timing was absolutely perfect," he said, "because even the government was saying, 'Wait a minute. Is this ever gonna end?' And thanks to the very creative writing of Barrett Strong, the lyrics never ever said what war was being talked about. It could've been the war in the neighborhood. It could've been the war in Southeast Asia. It simply said, 'War. What is it good for?'"

But, of course, it said substantially more than that. "War" had the most derisive grunt ever heard in song. One "Hunhhh!" was worth a thousand "Hell, no, we won't go"s.

Until 1969 a hundred percent of Motown's hit records were by black artists.

Then came Rare Earth Records, Motown's response to the Woodstock generation's impact on the pop music

War
By Norman Whitfield
and Barrett Strong

scene, the rise of albums, of self-contained bands, and of FM stations playing "progressive rock."

If this was the new sound of young America, Motown wanted in.

Having signed a white Detroit band called Rare Earth, Motown accepted their suggestion that the company start a new division for rock acts. Rare Earth Records issued albums by such bands as England's Pretty Things and by R. Dean Taylor, who co-wrote "Love Child" and scored a pop hit, "Indiana Wants Me," in 1970. Also on Rare Earth were Stoney and Meatloaf, the latter a singer who would go on to some fame in the late seventies. At Rare Earth he and Stoney covered the Temptations' "The Way You Do the Things You Do."

But it was Rare Earth, the band, that had the most success on the label. Their debut album, *Get Ready*, generated a hit single of the same name, followed by "(I Know) I'm Losing You" and "I Just Want to Celebrate." Rare Earth was a white band whose

members considered themselves "out in left field" at Motown. After all, they played their own instruments and sang their own songs.

But in fact, they fit right in with their hit records, and they even worked with Norman Whitfield, who by the late sixties had become Motown's designated producer of socially relevant records.

One of Whitfield's pet projects was the Undisputed Truth, which he put together in 1971, envisioning a "perfect cross between Sly Stone and the Fifth Dimension." He didn't get that, but he and Barrett Strong came up with "Smiling Faces Sometimes," a song about deception and paranoia that rang true in the Watergate era and became a hit.

Rare Earth Records was the best example of Motown's attempts to diversify in the seventies. The company reached out by making agreements to distribute records for companies recording music ranging from jazz and English rock and roll to South African trumpeter Hugh Masekela's Chisa label. In 1971 Motown had Sammy Davis, Jr., on its Ecology subsidiary. Other surprises on Motown's roster through the years: Billy Eckstine, Barbara McNair, Leslie Uggams, Diahann Carroll, Richard Pryor, Soupy Sales, Bobby Darin, Pat Boone. Boone was on Motown's country label, Melodyland Records, in 1975. By then Motown's management ranks were dominated by white executives, shown here at a trade association meeting. (Far left) The group Rare Earth.

SMOKEY ROBINSON
&
THE MIRACLES

*A*FTER fifteen years
with the Miracles, Smokey
Robinson announced that he
was leaving the group in 1972.

Actually, he'd wanted
to leave since 1969, when he'd
begun to sense that the other
members resented his top
billing and the additional
money he was earning as a
songwriter and as a vice
president at Motown.

At the same time
Robinson said he felt "used
and unappreciated" and was
tired of touring. But he
dragged out his departure
because he felt the group needed the money they earned from
concerts. In 1972 he declared
himself "burnt out." By then he
and his wife had two children,
including a newborn, and he
wanted to be home. Still he
stayed. Even after the Miracles
conducted a nationwide
replacement search and picked
Billy Griffin as their new lead
singer, Smokey agreed to a
farewell tour.

Retirement, of course,
was just a mirage. Within a
month, Robinson was considering Gordy's pleas to move to
Los Angeles, to help him with

(Left) One more time
for the "monkey see,
monkey do" routine from
"Mickey's Monkey." (Right)
Near the end of the road
for Smokey and the
Miracles. "Life on the
road was very hard," he
said. "I didn't want to be
away from my children
all the time. I didn't want
them to hardly know me.
That's why I decided it
was better to leave the
Miracles." The farewell
tour in 1972, Smokey said,
was "a time of turbulence
and tears. . . . I was being
bubbly for the fans, but
I was dying on the inside,
feeling like the character
in 'Tears of a Clown,'
smiling through my pain."

film projects – to be by his side, as always.

Soon Robinson was set up behind a desk in Motown's new Sunset Boulevard offices. After making two solo albums, he got restless. He'd found time to play golf; to be with his kids; to prowl L.A.'s clubs. He was bored. "I was happy but unhappy," he remembered, "just kind of dol-drumming away."

Robinson expressed his ambivalence in the album *A Quiet Storm* and began performing again.

But privately, it was a difficult time. Though he had a big hit with "Cruisin'" in 1979, his marriage was in trouble, and he fought a two-year battle with cocaine in the early eighties until, he says, "the Lord washed me clean."

The Miracles, meanwhile, were learning that where there was no Smokey, there was likely to be no fire.

A first album, *Renaissance*, went nowhere. A 1974 record, "Do It Baby," made the Top Twenty, but it wasn't until late 1975 that the Miracles were able to hit the top again, with a

Smokey, Diana, Marvin, and Stevie (not pictured) recorded a song for Pops Gordy's ninetieth birthday in 1978. (Above) In 1981 Smokey is surprised by an onstage visit from Berry Gordy, wishing him a happy twentieth anniversary in the music business. At an awards presentation for Smokey, Berry said: "As much as he thinks I have helped him, Smokey is one of the major reasons for my success. . . . Smokey, I love you." As he left the stage Berry couldn't help getting in a competitive snipe: "But I can also beat him in everything he's ever done!" Except, possibly, performing onstage.

driving dance number, "Love Machine," co-written by Pete Moore and Billy Griffin. The group then moved on to another company and disbanded in 1978.

"Sometimes I think things just burn themselves out," said Moore. "The magic days, they were with Smokey. After he left, it was still good for us, but how could it ever be better? Every magic has its time and place."

Certainly, Berry Gordy never doubted the extraordinary talents of his longtime friend and collaborator. When a high school student once asked Gordy, "How do you find guys like Smokey Robinson?" Gordy shot back, "We don't *find* guys like Smokey Robinson."

Bob Dylan called Smokey Robinson one of America's greatest living poets. The Beatles, the Rolling Stones, Linda Ronstadt, and Terence Trent D'Arby are among the dozens who've recorded his songs. And when the audience at the Rock and Roll Hall of Fame ceremonies interrupted his induction speech by serenading him with "Ooh, Baby, Baby," Smokey knew he had made it. "When you're writing a song," he once said, "you hope that people are going to sing it forever and ever." (Left) Smokey and Claudette had two children, a son born in 1968, Berry (named after Smokey's best friend), and a daughter born in 1970, Tamla, named after a lucky label.

DESPITE his talent – even genius – Marvin Gaye was an unhappy man constantly at war with himself and with others.

In 1972 he was riding high on *What's Going On*, an album that Gordy at first hated but that the public would love. It was a radical departure from the Motown sound. Gaye, with arranger David Van DePitte, the Funk Brothers, and many others, produced a finely woven album that soul-searched love and hatred, war and peace, spirituality, ecology, poverty, and our children's future.

"Marvin surprised us," said Smokey Robinson. "He seduced us with a new sound, funky as all hell, that soared with spirituality." Gaye, he said, had set a new standard.

When Gordy heard the album, he disagreed. He didn't think it was commercial enough, and Motown resisted releasing it. Gaye recalled the general consensus at the company: "Whew! Boy's really had it!" The album, however, sold two million copies and established Gaye as a serious artist. But as much as he

Marvin Gaye on the creation of *What's Going On*: "I conceived every bit of the music . . . . I can't write music, can't read music. But I was able to transmit my thoughts to another person, and David Van DePitte, through the graces of God, had enough talent to be able to receive it and put it on paper for me . . . but I'm gonna learn how to write music, so I can do it. Why? Because I want all the credit." (Right) Marvin conducts bass player Wilton Felder.

wanted stardom, Gaye hated the process; he resisted any appearance of selling out, and he remained uncomfortable onstage. He had stayed off, in fact, since the tragic death in 1970 of his occasional singing partner, Tammi Terrell.

His marriage to Anna Gordy had, over the years, become an unhappy one, and he increasingly turned to drugs for solace and escape.

The son of a disturbed and tyrannical father, Gaye had grown up plagued by insecurity and self-doubt. "My wife says I'm trying to prove I'm a man," Gaye once said, "and she's probably right." In 1971, at age thirty-two, he was talking about becoming a professional football player. Or a boxer.

In 1973 Gaye met Janis Hunter, seventeen years his junior. She inspired the sensuous album *Let's Get It On.*

Four years later his bitter divorce from Anna was finalized – and he commented on it on the album *Here, My Dear.* By 1980, despite numerous hits, Gaye had been forced to flee to England and Belgium to avoid back taxes and alimony.

When Marvin didn't even get nominated for a Grammy for *What's Going On* in 1972, he couldn't hide his feelings. "It's human to get hurt if you feel you deserve something and you don't get it," he said. "I've swept several awards this year, but I really want the Grammy. Not that I'm not happy with the others. I'm just . . . cocky . . . or selfish. Maybe that's the word." He finally won a Grammy in 1983, after he left the Motown label. (Left) Marvin at the Grammys in Los Angeles in 1977.

Mother, mother,

there's too many of you c r y i n g.

In 1982, having signed with CBS Records, he returned with a hit, "Sexual Healing."

Early in 1984, at the NBA all-star game, Gaye turned the "Star-Spangled Banner" into a soul-stirred love ballad. He could do anything with any song.

Personally, however, he was deeply troubled, and on April 1 of that year, a violent family argument ended with his father shooting Marvin dead.

Gaye's death, one day short of his forty-fifth birthday, threw Motown into grief. Berry Gordy called him the greatest entertainer of his time.

"The closest person I can relate him to is Billie Holiday," he said. "And I even consider Marvin better."

Marvin regularly hit the punching bags at a local boxing gym, and he described himself as a sports nut. "I even played hockey the other day," he said in 1973, and laughed. "Can you imagine a black man playing hockey?" He recalled a friend saying to him, "You're already one of the great musicians around town. Do you have to be the black George Plimpton also?" "Yes, I do," Gaye replied. "Quite frankly, yes." (Left) Marvin Gaye poses in a less athletic mood for the cover art on his album *What's Going On.*

Brother, brother, brother,

there's far too many of you d y i n g .

What's Going On
By Marvin Gaye,
Al Cleveland and
Renaldo Benson

I've been really t r y i n ', baby,

tryin' to hold back this feelin' for so long

and if you feel

like I feel, b a b y,

then *come on,*

oh come on.

Ooh, let's get it on.

Ow, baby,

let's get it on.

Let's Get It On
By Marvin Gaye and
Ed Townsend

Young women dancers often toured with Marvin after 1974. (Right) Marvin startled his audiences in the early eighties when he shaved his head. "Touring always tears at my guts," Marvin said. "Then I get out there and try to act like every woman's lost lover so she'll go out and buy three more copies of my latest record. Be serious! Is this me? How in the name of a just God did I ever turn myself into a sex god? And why?"

ɴ the early days of 1971, as he approached his twenty-first birthday, Stevie Wonder began to think about leaving home. He'd been with Motown for eleven years. He'd grown up at Hitsville, learned about the music business, met stars, and became one himself. Now he was restless, wary of ending up in a rut at Motown, upset about the company's move to Los Angeles. "It's very difficult to keep a relationship," he said, "when people are living in different parts of the world."

Though Wonder announced that he was leaving and fielded offers from other labels, in the end he stayed with Motown and with what he perceived to be a special kind of family. "Motown has done something for black history," he said, adding: "I felt the idea, the feeling behind this black company, gave a lot of black people a lot to be happy and thankful about."

Wonder was not acting on sentiment alone. He returned on his terms, spelled out in a 120-page contract that gave him financial security (with a higher royalty rate than

A slogan Motown came up with for Stevie in 1970 – "If you liked the boy, you'll love the man" – may have been clumsy, but there was no getting around it. Little Stevie had grown up – physically, musically, politically, and spiritually. In the early 1970s he began exploring his African heritage, which was reflected in changes in his musical sound.

When he turned twenty-
one, Stevie took a million
dollars of his accumulated
earnings from Motown
and invested much of it
in the future of his music.
He wanted to grow
musically, and, in the
electronic synthesizer,
he found a perfect tool.
Although the emerging
technology seemed
inhuman, Stevie
explained: "The way you
play an instrument has
a lot to do with [your]
character. . . . You can
really get into feeling
people through their
music. It's like the
synthesizer is a . . .
friend."

In 1970 Stevie and Syreeta Wright, a secretary at Motown who wanted to sing, began to write songs together. His affection for her inspired "Signed, Sealed, Delivered (I'm Yours)," and in September of that year they married in a Detroit church ceremony. The marriage lasted less than two years — Stevie blamed it on their stubborn personalities — but they stayed friends. Stevie produced Syreeta's first two Motown albums, and for awhile they shared the same hairstyle.

'Cause there's a place in the *s u n*

where there's hope

for ev'ryone,

where my *p o o r* restless heart's

gotta *r u n .*

Place in the Sun
By Bryan Wells

Motown had ever paid before) and control of the copyrights on his songs (Motown previously had owned the valuable rights to songs written by its artists and staff writers). Wonder demanded, and got, creative control. He could make records the way he wanted to, with whomever he wanted, on his own schedule. In short, he had forced Motown into modern times.

Wonder himself had vaulted onto the cutting edge of contemporary music by way of a recent discovery: the electronic synthesizer. The ability to program the sound of almost any instrument – and almost any sound he could conceive – freed him from the confines of Motown's studios and from session musicians. He became Motown's first self-contained artist. "It's just another dimension," he said. He was still interested, though, in acoustic instruments and in exploring sounds from Africa and Asia. Wonder's expanding musical vision would surface on albums like *Talking Book*, *Innervisions*, *Fulfillingness' First Finale*, and *Songs in the Key of Life.*

Stevie signs a new and very grown-up contract with Motown at a ceremony with Berry Gordy and Motown president Ewart Abner. In the early eighties Stevie devoted much of his energy to campaigning in Washington and around the country to have Martin Luther King's birthday declared a national holiday, which it was in 1983.

Stevie was in Washington again – and under arrest – on Valentine's Day 1985, when he participated in a protest outside the South African embassy against "the barbaric policies of apartheid." Seven months later his album *In Square Circle* included "It's Wrong (Apartheid)."

You are the sunshine of my l i f e,

that's why I'll always be a r o u n d.

For Wonder the eighties were full of hits, awards, and dreams come true. The young man who had been so influenced by the Beatles and Bob Dylan recorded a duet with Paul McCartney ("Ebony and Ivory") and wound up coaching Dylan on his part for the song "We Are the World."

He also threw himself into the successful campaign to have Martin Luther King, Jr.'s birthday declared a national holiday.

Wonder continues to create songs in the key of life, and he continues to do his work from his first and only home: Motown. The company may have changed over the years, but for him it remains a symbol of what blacks can do. As he puts it: "There is nothing wrong with being part of an achievement of your culture."

**You Are the Sunshine
of My Life**
By Stevie Wonder

Of all the turning points in his life, the most important was an automobile accident in North Carolina in 1973 that left Stevie in a comatose state for almost a week. "I was never the same," he said. "It taught me about life and death, and it all came out in my music from that point on . . . . The reason I push myself, and so intensely, is because I know that tomorrow is promised to no man."

The
MOTOWN
ALBUM

Stacy Lattisaw (above) has Motown roots of sorts. Her mother, Sondra, was lead singer in a Washington, D.C., high school group called the D.C. Tones; Marvin Gaye was a group member. Stacy herself scored a hit as a teenager with "Let Me Be Your Angel" in 1980. She joined Motown in 1986 and announced her arrival with a dance hit, "Nail It to the Wall." (Right) The Mary Jane Girls favored lace and corsets – onstage. Rick James formed the group and produced their first hit, "In My House." From left: Candi, Cheri, JoJo, Maxi.

There may never be
another Supremes, but
there also was no other
group like the Pointer
Sisters from Oakland,
whose songs ranged from
vintage jazz and country
(the Grammy-winning
"Fairytale") to Springsteen
("Fire") to dance classics
("Jump" and "I'm So
Excited"). From left:
Ruth, Anita, June.

Her name is Joyce Irby,
and she's new to
Motown, but, as
Fenderella, she's familiar
to fans of Klymaxx, with
whom she sang the hits
"The Men All Pause" and
"I Miss You" in 1985. Now
she's hip-hopped to
Motown, where she
mixes slam-jam dance
tracks with tender
ballads. (Below) The
Good Girls — from left,
Joyce T., Shireen C., and
De Monica S. — also
blend love songs with
percolating numbers such
as the Supremes'
"Love Is Like an Itching
in My Heart."

Oɴᴇ day in 1978, Rick James strutted into the Motown building in Hollywood and thumbed his nose at what was then about eighteen years of tradition.

He had a complete album in his hands, and it pulsed with something he called punk funk – nasty, streetwise noise about sex, drugs, and rock and roll. James loved to dress as outrageously as possible, looking like some Masai warrior from outer space with his chest bare and his hair in long, beaded braids.

He wanted total control of his music – from writing and producing to singing and playing. He wanted to be Stevie Wonder without paying the dues – and Berry Gordy said yes.

Rick James, of course, had advantages. For one thing, he was a nephew of the Tempts' Melvin Franklin. For another, he'd been at Motown before, back in the mid-sixties, with a band called the Mynah Birds. Besides James, the group included future members of Steppenwolf and Buffalo Springfield, including Neil

When he saw Berry Gordy in 1978, Rick James recalled, "I played him the tapes of 'You and I' and 'Mary Jane' and all that stuff, and Berry Gordy didn't halfway understand it, but he said, 'Okay.'" Berry understood more than Rick thought. "You and I" hit the top of the R&B charts, and his 1981 album, *Street Songs*, gave up two big hits, "Give It to Me Baby" and "Super Freak." "I'm into rock," James said. "I'm trying to change the root of funk, trying to make it more progressive, more melodic, and more lyrically structured. More honest, as opposed to putting riffs together, saying, 'Get up and get down. I feel all right. Oomph! Good God! Get up and boogie' and all that redundant bull." (Left) Rick James makes a point during his performance at a Farm Aid concert.

She's a super freak, super freak, she's super freaky

Super Freak
By Rick James and
Alonzo Miller

Young. They cut a few sides, but nothing was released, in part because James was in trouble with the military. When the band broke up, James moved to England but kept in touch with Motown. Now, in 1978, he was offering the company a chance to update the Sound of Young America by way of the funk scene.

James's material was often rude and crude; women were sex toys ("Super Freak"), and the younger the better ("17"). Drugs were fun ("Mary Jane"), and life was one long overnight party. The critics didn't like it, but his music sold in the millions.

James soon began working with other acts, including a group he created, the Mary Jane Girls (he wrote and produced their 1984 hit, "In My House"). The next year, he worked with his uncle's group ("Standing on the Top" on the Temptations' 1982 reunion album) and with Smokey Robinson, with whom he sang a duet in "Ebony Eyes" in 1984. Punk funk or not, once a Motowner, always a Motowner.

ONE of Motown's biggest hits in 1987 was by Bruce Willis, the raspy-voiced white guy from the TV show "Moonlighting."

Well, why not? Willis said he had always dug blues harmonica and Motown. "Just playing music is its own reward," he said. "It wouldn't have mattered to me if the album had made ten cents." In fact, *The Return of Bruno* sold a million copies, and the single "Respect Yourself" made it to Number Five. Not bad for a moonlighter.

Teena Marie was already signed to Motown when she got discovered.

She was on the Gordy roster without any records released when Rick James heard her voice piercing a studio wall at Motown.

He offered to be her producer and wrote "I'm a Sucker for Your Love," which she sent to the Top Ten of the R&B charts in 1979.

"I've always enjoyed black music," she said. "I should say that I've *lived* black music."

Teena Marie's picture wasn't on the cover of her first album, she said, "because I'm white." She added: "It was probably the right decision." In its early years, when Motown issued some albums (by the Miracles, the Marvelettes, Mary Wells, and the Isley Brothers) with cartoons and images of whites on the covers, many critics felt it was because the company was trying to get past racist record distributors. Smokey Robinson disputed that, though: "There was nothing to hide. We were just looking for devices to attract attention."

Bruce Willis was no musical threat to a certain other Bruce, but he had his moment. "Respect Yourself," the Staple Singers' staple, landed him in the Top Ten.

DeBARGE

DeBarge (left) was Motown's family act for the eighties. From left: James, El, Bunny, Randy, Mark. In 1982 the group had a gold album, *All This Love*, but their biggest record came in 1985. "Rhythm of the Night," which was on the soundtrack of the karate movie *Berry Gordy's The Last Dragon*, hit the Top Ten. El DeBarge (above left) emerged as a solo star in 1986 with the hit "Who's Johnny." And James DeBarge had a moment in the spotlight when he married Janet Jackson in 1984. The marriage didn't last. Johnny Gill (right) and Gerald Alston (above) are determined that the music of the nineties won't be overwhelmed by drum machines and synthesizers. Johnny stepped into the solo spotlight from the youthful New Edition, to which he still belongs, while Gerald is a veteran of seventeen years with the Manhattans, who won a 1981 Grammy for "Shining Star." At Motown, Gerald is introducing new soul – a mix of some of his strongest influences, including Sam Cooke, Jackie Wilson, Teddy Pendergrass, and, of course, gospel music.

The
M O T O W N
A L B U M

In the early sixties it was Little Stevie. In the early seventies it was the Jackson 5. In the early eighties it was DeBarge. Now, at the dawn of the nineties, it looks like the Boys.

With their 1989 hit, "Dial My Heart," the Boys, four brothers from California, grabbed hold of a Motown legacy, and they are well aware of it.

"Once we wanted to be just like the Jacksons," said Khiry Abdul-Samad, oldest of the Boys. (At the time of their first hit, Khiry was fifteen; Hakeem, thirteen; Tajh, eleven; and Bilal, nine.) The Boys lip-synched to Jackson 5 albums and copied Michael's dance steps from videos. Early on, they earned comparisons with both the Jacksons and New Edition. But now, says Khiry, "We know we can be ourselves. We have our own styles and our own personalities."

That sounds like the future talking.

The Boys got their start performing on the beach in Venice, California, to raise money for a Father's Day gift. When they counted up sixty-nine dollars for a few hours of singing, their parents allowed them to become regulars at the beach. At one performance they sang between a chainsaw juggler act and a one-man band. Eventually, the Boys got a Motown contract. (Left) The Boys perform at 1989's Soul-by-the-Sea concert in Jamaica. From left: Hakeem, Bilal, Tajh, Khiry.

*I*N 1988 Berry Gordy sold Motown Records to MCA, keeping his publishing and film-production divisions. He observed: "Now that everyone not only has a mind of their own but also an attorney's and an agent's mind as well, it's not the same atmosphere." But if some critics have complained that the old Motown and the Motown Sound are dead, you won't find Smokey Robinson among the mourners. The Motown Sound, he says, "was a young sound created by a bunch of young people at a certain place and time. We got older, we got married, had babies, moved away. Expecting us to keep that same sound would be like expecting us to stay nineteen forever."

It's not that anyone expected the company to maintain the breathtaking pace of its first decade, when, in 1966, three out of four releases made the national charts, and when, one week in 1968, Motown artists had five of the country's Top Ten records. But over the years Motown established itself as one of the most successful black-owned enterprises in

(Left) Lionel Richie had a twin win at the Grammys in 1985, when *Can't Slow Down* won album of the year, and Richie and co-producer James Anthony Carmichael tied for producer of the year with David Foster. All the Commodores dreamt about the Grammys. "When we put out an album, man, all we could think about was a Number One song," Lionel said, "and which row we were gonna sit in at the Grammys." (Right) Stevie Wonder, one of Motown's most honored artists, adds one more — a gold record for *In Square Circle* in 1985.

American history, and it has continued to produce hits.

After the first golden era, the record-sellers included the Commodores, Rick James, DeBarge, the Dazz Band, Bruce Willis, Rockwell, Charlene, the Mary Jane Girls, and the Boys.

Sometimes the biggest hits are the oldest, in new hands. New artists cover Hitsville classics: among others, UB40 performing "The Way You Do the Things You Do," Phil Collins resurrecting "You Can't Hurry Love," and Cyndi Lauper singing "What's Going On." Motown survives, and, considering the brutality and volatility of the record business, it's a miracle. In fact, the real magic is that Motown never went away – when *The Big Chill* opened with the sounds of Marvin Gaye singing "I Heard It through the Grapevine," it reminded an entire generation of the music's initial strength and of its enduring power. The music is within us forever – and so are its makers.

One of Marvin Gaye's last appearances was for "Motown 25." In May 1983

Marvin Gaye's "I Heard It through the Grapevine" went to Number One on both the pop and soul charts and sold four million copies when it was released in 1968. Helping him with some of the gold records is Barney Ales, who began as a friend and advisor to Motown's billing department in 1959 and became a company sales vice president. (Below) The Jacksons get a load of gold for their cleverly titled *Third Album* in 1970.

In 1974 Stevie Wonder, who has won sixteen Grammys, took home five for his work on *Talking Book* and *Innervisions*. Stevie celebrates backstage with, from left, Little Richard, Lula Mae Hardaway (Stevie's mother), and Chuck Berry. Hardaway encouraged Stevie to pursue music and is credited as a co-writer on several songs, including "I Was Made to Love Her" and "Signed, Sealed, Delivered (I'm Yours)." This was Stevie's way of thanking her for cooking during songwriting sessions at his house and tossing in suggestions on various songs.

he was an unhappy man, but, like so many others from the early years of Hitsville, he'd come home.

Now, dressed in an elegant white suit and seated at a grand piano, he traced the historical roots of the Motown Sound back to wooden churches and gospel choirs, to slavery and folk songs, to heat and hurting. "Yesterday was the birth of today," he said, and today is "guy-and-girl songs, songs of protest and anger, songs of gentleness and songs of wounds left unattended for far too long. It's songs to dance to, it's songs to march to, to fly to, to make love to. It's music pure and simple. . . . Full of promise and determination, unity and humanity."

He put his palms together and gazed into the audience. "My loved ones," he said softly, "today is the birth-place of forever."

In May 1982 Diana Ross was the 1,747th entertainer to get her star along the Hollywood Walk of Fame, in front of 6712 Hollywood Boulevard. Smokey Robinson followed in 1983 as star number 1,759 (at 1500 North Vine). Claudette is by his side, though they divorced a few years later.

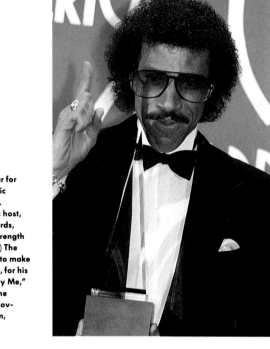

Lionel Richie's year for the American Music Awards was 1985. Besides serving as host, he took in six awards, primarily on the strength of "Hello." (Below) The next year, he had to make room for an Oscar, for his song "Say You, Say Me," the title song for the Mikhail Baryshnikov-Gregory Hines film, *White Nights*.

(Above) Stevie had to fight off a plagiarism suit over the song in 1990, but in 1985 he was reveling in his first Oscar – for "I Just Called to Say I Love You" from the film *The Woman in Red*. Berry and Robert Gordy, former vice president of Jobete Publishing, with Stevie Wonder. (Left) Jheryl Busby, current president of Motown Records, receives the NAACP President's Award in 1989.

The
MOTOWN
ALBUM

Motown artists helped celebrate the Apollo Theatre's fiftieth anniversary in 1985 with an NBC television special. Guests included (left) Rod Stewart, Gregory Hines, and Marilyn McCoo, who joined (right) Diana Ross, Stevie Wonder, Smokey Robinson, Patti LaBelle, and George Michael, among many others, for the finale.

The
M O T O W N
A L B U M

The Four Tops – from left, Obie, Levi, Duke, Lawrence – were inducted into the Rock and Roll Hall of Fame in 1990 along with the team responsible for most of their – and Motown's – greatest hits, Lamont Dozier, Brian Holland, and Eddie Holland, shown here (far right) with Diana Ross.

(Far left) The Temptations reunite in 1989 to be inducted into the Hall of Fame. Eddie is at the podium; David stands behind Melvin Franklin and in front of Otis and Dennis. (Left) At his induction the same year, Stevie with his two children Kieta and Aisha.

The man who started it all is inducted in January 1988. Gordy told the audience: "I would like to thank a country whose form of government makes it possible for someone to have a dream like mine come true." But he admitted, "I still like it behind the scenes better."

Marvin Gaye was inducted into the Rock and Roll Hall of Fame posthumously. In 1987 Anna Gordy Gaye, whose marriage to him inspired both his most joyous and his most sadly reflective music, accepts the honor, accompanied by their son, Marvin Pentz Gaye III. Berry Gordy said, "Truest to his art was Marvin Gaye. His life was in every song."

In May 1983, Motown was going on twenty-five when it produced a special on NBC, "Motown 25: Yesterday, Today, Forever." The show hit several emotional and musical peaks, swept the ratings, and earned an Emmy for outstanding variety program. Richard Pryor (above), standing at "the machine in Hitsville that cut million-seller records," introduces Smokey Robinson and the Miracles (joined by Claudette for the occasion), while (right) Martha Reeves and Mary Wells reprise their biggest hits. At evening's end Berry Gordy greets his galaxy of stars, among them the Temptations, the Tops, the Supremes, the Jacksons, Marvin Gaye, and Stevie Wonder.

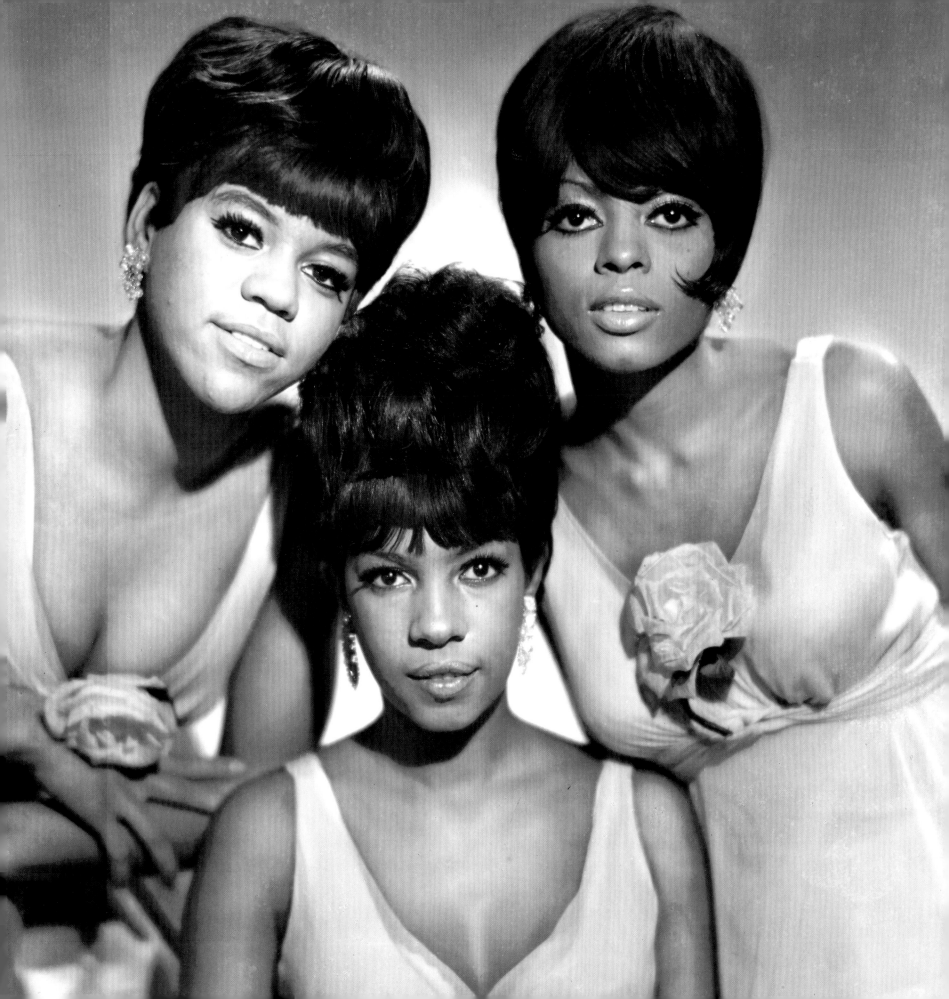

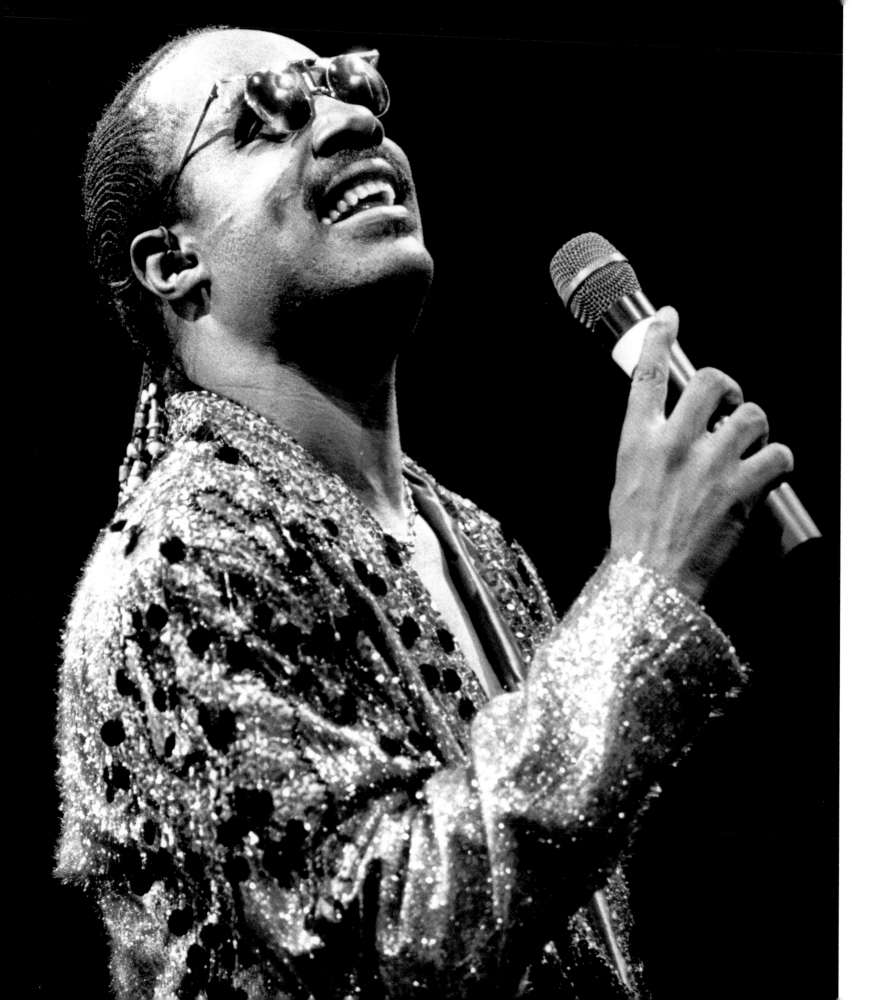

A Critical Discography of the Motown Era, 1959–1989

*S*MOKEY Robinson once told me that, as Motown records began to crowd the top of the charts in the mid-sixties, producers from all over the country began to crowd into Detroit, hoping to produce their own version of the "Motown Sound." They couldn't rent Motown's funky little recording studio, but they often managed to hire the same session musicians Motown used, even the immortal rhythm section of bassist James Jamerson and drummer Benny Benjamin. But few, if any, hits resulted, and none of them sounded like Motown anyway. In the meantime, the Gordy group itself kept releasing hits, three or four a month, more hits than any other record label before or since.

Motown's production approach has been described as an assembly line. And it was. But the lines of a vintage Mustang can be as appealing in their own right as those of a Matisse. The mistake made by those outside producers – and a generation of historians and critics after them – was to believe in a monolithic Motown Sound that never existed. It's a myth. There were some stylistic elements that many Motown records, particularly in the mid-sixties, had in common. But the records produced by Berry Gordy, Smokey Robinson, Holland-Dozier-Holland, and Norman Whitfield each represent such distinct styles, are so different from one another, that they take no special perspicacity to apprehend – unless you happen to think there's no big difference between the Contours' "Do You Love Me," Mary Wells's "My Guy," the Four Tops'

Produced by
BERRY GORDY, Jr.

"Reach Out I'll Be There," and Marvin Gaye's "I Heard It through the Grapevine." They're all definitive examples of the Motown Sound, as different as the men and women who wrote and sang and arranged and recorded them.

Once you begin to delve into the depths of the Motown story, what impresses you most is the delicious particularity of each of those records. If Motown is as much the story of Jamerson's bass lines and Eddie Holland's lyrics as it is of Diana Ross's vocals and Smokey Robinson's songs, it is more than anything the product of the moments in which several of those distinguished components came together. Just listen to the opening seconds of the Temptations' "My Girl," in which the archetypal Jamerson bass line sets up the perfection of Robinson's rhymes within the rasping ache of David Ruffin's voice. Which is not to slight the gorgeous harmonies the rest of the Tempts provide, or Benjamin's driving drum rolls, or some of the sharpest finger pops in the history of recorded sound. By the time Ruffin gets 'round to declaring "I've got all the riches, baby, one man can claim," the listener feels as wealthy as Ruffin.

And "My Girl" is by no means the greatest example of what any of these men contributed to the Motown Sound. Essentially, the same crew came back only six months later with "Since I Lost My Baby," which features even more yearning power and an even more elegant arrangement.

Motown was the greatest record production center in history. When preparing this discography, I planned to include only the most relevant examples, figuring a hundred records would do it. In the end I selected more than 250 and felt as though I'd had to leave a few things out. There is no other record label about which such a claim could seriously be made.

Motown's music developed through several distinct phases. Rather than organize this discography by artist, producer, songwriter, or chart history, I've chosen to divide the company's history into relevant but somewhat arbitrary periods: The years before the big national breakout, 1959–1963; the soulful glory days of the mid-sixties, 1964–1967; the pop heyday, 1968–1970; the years of change and movement away from both Detroit and the sixties idea of soul, 1970–1975; the disco/funk period, 1976–1980; and the eighties, when the creative community around which Motown had been centered disintegrated, although the making and marketing of good music did not.

I've avoided discussing anthology albums, because the repackaging of the greater and lesser Motown hits would make for a fascinating, if somewhat bewildering, book in itself. However, it would be unfair to pretend that I don't have my favorites among Motown anthologies or that they weren't what I listened to while I wrote. In fact, one of the records that first made me want to write about rock and soul music was *A Collection of 16 Original Big Hits, Volume 2* (now available as Motown CD MOTD 5449), which I've been listening to at least once a month for the past twenty-seven years. It contains some of the real wonders of the early Motown years, including Eddie Holland's unbelievable Jackie Wilson impression on "Leaving Here," a rock-and-roll fable Chuck Berry could envy; the Temptations' jumping pre-David Ruffin "I Want a Love I Can See"; the Contours' house-rocking "Shake Sherry"; the Valadiers' prepolitical "Greetings (This Is Uncle Sam)"; the Miracles' bittersweet "I Gotta Dance to Keep from Crying"; and the Supremes' hilarious and lascivious nonhit "Buttered Popcorn," possibly the most sensual record they ever made and the only one on which Florence Ballard ever sang lead. *The 64 Greatest Motown Hits*, the CIMCO TV-advertised collection, another set I've listened to obsessively ever since I first bought it (about 1972, in the Cunningham's drugstore at Thirteen Mile and Woodward in Detroit), is the single best overview of the Motown story up to the Jackson 5 and Rare Earth that I've ever found.

But no anthology has everything. For instance, as far as I know, Carolyn Crawford's gorgeous "My Smile Is Just a Frown Turned Upside Down" remains unanthologized. But that's an endless game.

There has been no end to the pleasures to be taken from these records. And I speak from experience. Motown has offered me release and relaxation, insight and support in dark hours. To this music and the people who made it, I can pay no greater tribute than to quote from one of its grandest achievements: "It makes my burden a little bit lighter / Makes my life a little bit brighter / 'Cause you're a wonderful one" (Marvin Gaye, "Wonderful One").

1959–1963

Money (That's What I Want), Barrett Strong, Tamla 54027, 1959 (also issued on Anna 1111 for distribution outside Detroit)
Do You Love Me, The Contours, Gordy 7005, 1962

The Motown story inevitably begins with Berry Gordy, Jr., the man whose drive and vision established the company as the most successful black-owned business enterprise in American history. But to understand Gordy only as the most brilliant entrepreneur of the black middle class is to shortchange his accomplishments. By the time he founded Motown, he already was the most musically accomplished record company owner in America. Gordy licensed sides to other labels such as Marv Johnson's "Come to Me" and "You Got What It Takes" (both issued on United Artists) and the Miracles' "Bad Girl," issued on Chess, and "Got a Job," issued on End Records. At Motown, Gordy both wrote and produced the company's first smashes, "Money" and "Do You Love Me," with their powerhouse piano, bass, drums, and raucous R&B vocals.

As if there were – somewhere in Memphis or Los Angeles or New York – a record industry maven devoted to the cause of Art against Mammon, "Money," the company's first hit, is conventionally understood as a metaphor for Motown's existence. This misses the point, which is that "Money" spoke for the ambitions of an entire generation. "The best things in life are free / But you can keep 'em for the birds'n'bees" may earn the contempt of contemporary boho liberals, but don't forget how easily the Love Crowd succumbed to the temptations of the Big Chill. And anyway, that's all in the eye of the beholder, since – dare I say it? – the frantic beat suggests that what Gordy really had concocted was something of a philosophical jest.

In any event, "Money" was not the sum and substance of the Motown philosophy. The other side of the coin is represented by "Do You Love Me," a song equally as passionate but about dancing and romance. Billy Gardner's inimitable spoken introduction sets up this 2:49 blast of pure energy as a story of revenge and rebellion. Together with the fools-'em-every-time false ending, it stands out as a light-hearted example of the same dramatic sense that informs classic Motown from "Reach Out I'll Be There" to "Let's Get It On." The animating emotion isn't greed but lust. And that makes "Do You Love Me," like "Money," rock and roll as pure as anybody ever made it.

Shop Around, The Miracles, Tamla 54034, 1960

The greatest love affair in Motown history may have been the friendship between Berry Gordy, Jr., and his first protege, William "Smokey" Robinson. With their third release together, Motown scored its first million seller, though not without a creative struggle. "Shop Around," which opens with a breathless recitation by Smokey that echoes the one in "Got a Job," the first record he and Gordy made together, originally was recorded at a slower tempo, with more prominent sax and guitar accompaniment – a more typical rhythm and blues approach to making a harmony group record. But a few weeks after its release, Berry phoned Smokey in the middle of the night, insisting that he gather up the rest of the Miracles and get to the studio – at 3 a.m. They recut the record with a slightly lighter groove. For Robinson, whose gifts were closer to those of Jackie Wilson and Johnny Mathis than to the rawer voices of contemporary soul, it was a career-making decision. For Motown, it was an ace launching pad.

Two Lovers, Mary Wells, Motown 1035, 1962
You Lost the Sweetest Boy, Mary Wells, Motown 1048, 1963
My Guy, Mary Wells, Motown 1056, 1964

Wells was Motown's first great female star, scoring ten consecutive Top Ten R&B hits (four in the pop Top Ten) between January 1961 and "My Guy" in April 1964. Her records, with their mix of brassy assertion and breathy vulnerability over light, tight grooves, set the pattern for the later triumphs of Martha Reeves and Diana Ross. Wells wasn't quite as powerful a singer as Martha, and she certainly didn't

possess any of Ross's iconic charisma, but the records she made with Smokey Robinson are first-rate examples of the Motown groove in its formative stages. "My Guy" (which I've snuck in here despite the fact that its release date was a couple of months over the line) gives a strong sense of Robinson's developing abilities, and "Two Lovers" is one of his first great shaggy-dog soap operas.

Motown's future was more clearly spelled out by "You Lost the Sweetest Boy." Ostensibly the B side of "What's Easy for Two Is So Hard for One," it outcharted "What's Easy" on the pop charts. And "You Lost the Sweetest Boy" was written and produced not by Smokey Robinson but by Eddie and Brian Holland and Lamont Dozier.

Way over There, The Miracles, Tamla 54028, 1960
Jamie, Eddie Holland, Motown 1021, 1961
Buttered Popcorn, The Supremes, Tamla 54045, 1961
Mind over Matter, The Pirates, Melody 105, 1962
Hitch Hike, Marvin Gaye, Tamla 54075, 1962
Can I Get a Witness, Marvin Gaye, Tamla 54087, 1963
I Want a Love I Can See, The Temptations, Gordy 7015, 1963
Leavin' Here, Eddie Holland, Motown 1052, 1963
Come and Get These Memories, Martha and the Vandellas, Gordy 1014, 1963

On "Way over There," the Miracles created a perfect approximation of fifties doo-wop harmony as practiced by Nolan Strong and the Diablos, among others. So perfect that when the first rock and roll revival rolled around, the record was reissued and charted nationally two years after it initially flopped.

By 1962 rock and roll was glowing with its brush with premature nostalgia, setting the stage for "Come and Get These Memories," the only Motown hit sentimental enough to have been a Phil Spector's Wall of Sound girl-group side. Sentimentality, however, proved a most un-Motown-like trait.

The Supremes, gritless though they were, could never have been a Spectorian girl group. "Buttered Popcorn," one of their earliest singles, is a pure novelty. Florence Ballard praises her favorite theatrical comestible as "greasy . . . and gooey . . . and sticky . . . and salty" so effusively that after awhile you kinda have to wonder if she isn't inhabiting the wonderful land of metaphor. Diana Ross soon took over and transcended – or was that sublimated? – all such thoughts.

Eddie Holland, who'd begun his career singing on Berry Gordy, Jr.'s demonstration tapes for Jackie Wilson, made several good records as a Wilson emulator. "Jamie" (written by neither Gordy nor Holland but by Mickey Stevenson and Barrett Strong) got the Wilson style down as sweetly and perfectly as it could be done, but "Leavin' Here," with its wondrous lyrical attack on male chauvinism, is more indicative of what the future held for Holland. Working with his brother Brian and another erstwhile performer, Lamont Dozier, Holland became part of one of the greatest writing/production teams of the sixties. "Leavin' Here" is one of their earliest masterpieces.

Before David Ruffin, the Tempts had tried a number of guises, including street harmony, as in the rocking "I Want a Love I Can See," whose complex vocal interchanges suggest their later style. But the Tempts weren't above poaching a rival's style, as in "Mind over Matter," which finds the group, a good two years before its national breakout, aping Nolan Strong and the Diablos – among the Motor City's more obscure local heroes – and on one of the Diablos' own numbers, to boot.

First marketed as a run-of-the-mill ballad smoothy of the Billy Eckstine/Nat "King" Cole type, Marvin Gaye began to find his own sound with up-tempo material like Holland-Dozier-Holland's gospel knockoff "Can I Get a Witness." But his real forte was some kind of middle way between the two approaches, as on the more polished road number "Hitch Hike," which he co-wrote with Clarence Paul – a former member of the 5 Royales and a key figure in Stevie Wonder's early career – and studio straw boss Stevenson.

Fingertips, part 2, Little Stevie Wonder, Tamla 54080, 1963

The real show here is Stevie himself, blistering ears with both harmonica and vocal, threatening to explode with delight. He'd been making records for a year already (notably "Contract of Love"), but here he found his stride as an exemplar of pure rhythmic joy.

Greetings (This Is Uncle Sam), The Valadiers, Miracle M6, 1961; The Monitors, VIP 25039, 1966
The Great March to Freedom, Reverend Martin Luther King, Gordy G-908, 1963

Another Motown myth worth dispelling is that the label eschewed politics. In fact, Gordy was involved in social issues right from the beginning – unless you construe the Miracles' "Got a Job" as some kind of hedonism. The Valadiers' "Greetings (This Is Uncle Sam)," covered five years later by the Monitors, is one of Motown's most pointed jokes. Its soaring doo-wop "I need youuuuu" drips sarcasm, and the hostility to military service is overt.

Perhaps this could all be described as prepolitical. But not *The Great March to Freedom*. Recorded at a Detroit rally, the album features one of the earliest versions of Dr. King's "Dream" speech. Its release confirmed both Motown's essential solidarity with the civil rights movement and Berry Gordy's great ear for talent. This is not only a great sermon but a compulsively listenable one.

Heat Wave, Martha and the Vandellas, Gordy 7022, 1963
The Miracles Doin' Mickey's Monkey, The Miracles, Tamla TM-245, 1963
When the Lovelight Starts Shining through His Eyes, The Supremes, Motown 1051, 1963

Here Holland-Dozier-Holland began to hit their stride as songwriters, producers, and visionaries. If Berry Gordy was the reigning genius at Motown, Brian Holland and Lamont Dozier most fully put the principles he established into practice. (Eddie Holland was never credited as part of the production team, but he was more than just its principal lyricist, working closely on the vocal arrangements as well.) H-D-H worked with just about every act on the label, but what defined their sound was the granite rhythmic base with gospel touches. This basic groove could be embellished. For instance, H-D-H crafted Motown's first great album from the Miracles, a group previously defined by its ballads, in the process coming up with Smokey's two best dance hits, "Mickey's Monkey" and "I Gotta Dance to Keep from Crying." "When the Lovelight Starts Shining through His Eyes" put the Supremes through similar paces and, not incidentally, effectively established Diana Ross as the group's central voice and H-D-H as her primary mentors.

But the real masterpiece of this period of the Motown story is "Heat Wave," a record whose groove amounts to obsession. It kicks off almost predictably, with bass, drum, and tambourine led by a rumbling baritone sax and a piano figure. Then Martha enters, and it's a new day. She sings of sexual desire in terms more intimate and explicit than any woman had ever dared to before. "Has high blood pressure got a hold on me, or is this the way love's supposed to be?" she asks. Without waiting for an answer, the music charges on, without pity.

Martha finds herself mystified by her own eroticism: "Sometimes I stare in space / Tears all over my face / I can't explain it, don't understand it, ain't never felt like this before." Behind her the Vandellas advise, "Go ahead, girl / Ain't nothin' but love, girl." "Don't pass up this chance," they go on to declare, "it sounds like a new romance." For "Heat Wave" is by any measure the greatest record of Motown's early years and the one that most clearly set the pace for the glory days that followed.

HONORABLE MENTION

Bye Bye Baby, Mary Wells, Motown 1003, 1960
You Can Depend on Me, The Miracles, Tamla 54028, 1960
Please Mr. Postman, The Marvelettes, Tamla 54046, 1961
What's So Good about Goodbye, The Miracles, Tamla 54053, 1961
Shake Sherry, The Contours, Gordy 7012, 1962
You Beat Me to the Punch, Mary Wells, Motown 1032, 1962
I'll Try Something New, The Miracles, Tamla 54059, 1962
Beechwood 4-5789, The Marvelettes, Tamla 54065, 1962

Stubborn Kind of Fellow, Marvin Gaye, Tamla 54068, 1962
You've Really Got a Hold on Me, The Miracles, Tamla 54073, 1962
Contract of Love, Little Stevie Wonder, Tamla 54074, 1962
Quicksand, Martha and the Vandellas, Gordy 7025, 1963
Pride and Joy, Marvin Gaye, Tamla 54079, 1963
Mickey's Monkey, The Miracles, Tamla 54083, 1963
I Gotta Dance to Keep from Crying, The Miracles, Tamla 54089, 1963
Castles in the Sand, Stevie Wonder, Tamla 54090, 1963

1964–1967

Dancing in the Street, Martha and the Vandellas, Gordy 7033, 1964
Nowhere to Run, Martha and the Vandellas, Gordy 7039, 1965

"Nowhere to Run" takes the eroticized passions of "Heat Wave" to their most paranoiac extreme; Benny Benjamin and James Jamerson never played with greater power or precision, and the result – thanks to H-D-H's hot hand – is one of the biggest-sounding records ever made.

"Dancing in the Street," put together by William "Mickey" Stevenson with some compositional help from Marvin Gaye, has some of the hottest drumming in Motown history, a great horn chart, and another of Martha's inimitable clarion vocals.

My Girl, The Temptations, Gordy 7038, 1964
Since I Lost My Baby, The Temptations, Gordy 7043, 1965

These records represent the opposite sides of Smokey Robinson's romantic vision, not to mention the apex of David Ruffin's singing career. Ruffin's growling slide out of the bridge into the verse of "Since I Lost My Baby" still strikes me as miraculous, and if James Jamerson was soon to play more complex bass lines, what he did here was to concoct one that forever defines a song and a feeling.

Where Did Our Love Go, The Supremes, Motown 1060, 1964
Baby Love, The Supremes, Motown 1066, 1964

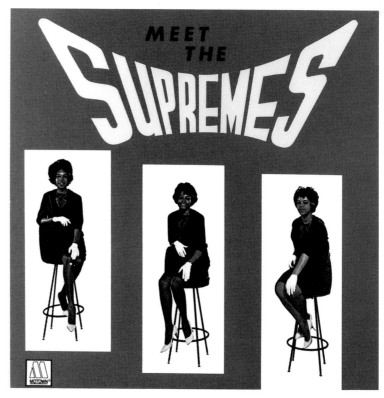

Come See about Me, The Supremes, Motown 1068, 1964
Stop! In the Name of Love, The Supremes, Motown 1074, 1965
Back in My Arms Again, The Supremes, Motown 1075, 1965
Nothing But Heartaches, The Supremes, Motown 1080, 1965

A one-year supply of Supremes' singles, from July 1964 to July 1965. The first five all hit Number One on the pop charts, a record no one's ever going to top.

By devoting herself in not-really-equal proportions to role-playing as much as singing technique, Diana Ross established a persona as maddening as it was fascinating, a persona that completely overwhelmed her group, let alone the competition. "Baby Love," one of the purest Ross vehicles, may strike you either as the most arch and aggravating hit record of the sixties or as one of the greatest examples of making something out of next-to-nothing. About the others there's less doubt. The Supremes' stage image may have been all frills and frivolity, but on the radio, they sent a different message. Ross's gasping desperation on "Come See about Me" grows progressively darker in "Stop! In the Name of Love."

The power of the music H-D-H created comes from the tension between Ross's relaxed singing, which luxuriates in its own legato phrasing, and the urgency of the rhythm section, whose throb heightens the anxiety, notch by notch, verse by verse. Even "Back in My Arms Again," which balances baritone sax and vibes, has its ominous side. Ross is reclaiming her guy because she's finally learned to listen to her own heart rather than follow her friends' advice. There's pleasure here, sure, but not anything you'd recognize as joy, let alone triumph.

"Nothing But Heartaches" completed the cycle but failed to top the charts – it *did* make Number Eleven – possibly because its melody was too close to "Back in My Arms Again." "I Hear a Symphony," which followed, really is a frivolous love tune, albeit a Bach rewrite. It, too, made Number One, one of ten chart-toppers the Supremes scored between 1964 and 1967.

The Greatest Hits/From the Beginning, The Miracles, Tamla TS2-254, 1965
The Four Tops' Second Album, The Four Tops, Motown MS-634, 1965
The Temptations Sing Smokey, The Temptations, Gordy G-912, 1965
Dance Party, Martha and the Vandellas, Gordy G-915, 1965

Three more arguments in favor of a Motown album aesthetic. Smokey's post-doo-wop romantic poetry is even better portrayed, though, on *The Temptations Sing Smokey*. Obviously, the finest things here are the hits – "My Girl," "The Way You Do the Things You Do," and "It's Growing" – but like all great albums, this one defined the styles of the people who made it.

So does *The Four Tops' Second Album*, which features three hits and such definitive nonthrowaways as "Helpless," "I Like Everything about You," and "Stay in My Lonely Arms," as well as the minor masterpiece "Love Feels Like Fire," which is as close as Holland-Dozier-Holland ever allowed themselves to come to the actual form of gospel music.

Dance Party is a kind of early concept album, featuring covers of other people's dance hits ("Mickey's Monkey," "The Jerk," "Hitch Hike") and program numbers like "Mobile Lil the Dancing Witch," which is – at least – no less worthy than "Lovely Rita Meter Maid." Besides "Dancing in the Street," "Wild One" (a minor hit), and "Nowhere to Run," the album features its own lost classic, the pulsing "Motoring."

Shotgun, Junior Walker and the All Stars, Soul 35008, 1965
(I'm a) Road Runner, Junior Walker and the All Stars, Soul 35015, 1966

Although his instrument was saxophone, not guitar, Walker was the most down home and bluesy of all the Motown stars, and "Road Runner," in particular, is stamped with country wisdom.

Devil with the Blue Dress, Shorty Long, Soul 35001, 1964
First I Look at the Purse, The Contours, Gordy 7044, 1965
Shake and Fingerpop, Junior Walker and the All Stars, Soul 35013, 1965
High-Heel Sneakers, Stevie Wonder, Tamla 54119, 1965
Beauty Is Only Skin Deep, The Temptations, Gordy 7055, 1966

Great art never has to take itself entirely seriously. Motown often released records that were wholly or partially humorous. Shorty Long's "Devil with the Blue Dress" is one long leer (later expropriated by Mitch Ryder and Bruce Springsteen, who rounded off its edges). "First I Look at the Purse" and "Beauty Is Only Skin Deep" are the other side of Motown romanticism – dated now by their sexism but providing a lot of amusement at the time.

"High-Heel Sneakers," a song that originated with the blues singer Tommy Tucker, has been a hit half a dozen times. But nobody ever energized

this account of the world's weirdest date better than Stevie Wonder.

"Shake and Fingerpop" works the same territory, only the final verse takes place on the dance floor at some weird shack where such exotic dress is as normal as the trilling and squawking of Walker's sax.

Ooo Baby Baby, The Miracles, Tamla 54113, 1965
The Tracks of My Tears, The Miracles, Tamla 54118, 1965
My Girl Has Gone, The Miracles, Tamla 54123, 1965
The Love I Saw in You Was Just a Mirage, Smokey Robinson and the Miracles, Tamla 54145, 1967

If Holland-Dozier-Holland's great hidden theme was the eroticism of despair, Smokey Robinson's turned out to be the ecstasy of secrecy. In this regard the very titles of "The Tracks of My Tears" and "The Love I Saw in You Was Just a Mirage" become pertinent. But even "Ooo Baby Baby," a song so perfectly attuned to courtship that Robinson has called it his "national anthem," finds him pleading to be forgiven for betrayal.

Robinson's heralded way with a metaphor makes him Motown's most famous lyricist, and he's certainly its most elegant. Who else would ever have thought to rhyme *mirage* with militaristic terms like *sabotage* and *camouflage*?

The Miracles' secret weapon, though, was guitarist Marv Tarplin, a great but unheralded instrumentalist in a league with James Jamerson and Benny Benjamin. On "My Girl Has Gone," it takes one of the most thundering productions Smokey ever concocted to keep Tarplin's creamy opening chords from stealing the show.

Uptight (Everything's Alright), Stevie Wonder, Tamla 54124, 1965
Nothing's Too Good for My Baby, Stevie Wonder, Tamla 54130, 1966
Someday at Christmas, Stevie Wonder, Tamla 54142, 1966
I Was Made to Love Her, Stevie Wonder, Tamla 54151, 1967

One reason that the total impression of Motown's music is stunning is that it seems to have been created by a community of obsessive zealots. So maybe it figures that it would have

Stevie Wonder, the blind teenage soul shouter, who sounded the most possessed *by* vision. In the great gospel tradition, the music seemed to inhabit him; he became a mere channel, almost sputtering out the choruses of "Uptight" and "Nothing's Too Good for My Baby."

"Someday at Christmas," released just after Wonder turned sixteen, is both the great lost Motown Christmas single and the first evidence he gave of having full control of his vision. Extraordinary human being though he is, even Stevie Wonder had to grow into his talent. Here, singing what ought to be nothing more than a seasonal homily, he made that corny message fresh and took it beyond cliché. But it was "I Was Made to Love Her," in musical respects very much a replay of "Uptight," that showed how much control Stevie had gained. His tendency to sputter remained, but this time, he used it for a wisely limited effect – pushing out "my papa dis-approved it."

It Takes Two, Marvin Gaye and Kim Weston, Tamla 54141, 1966
Ain't No Mountain High Enough, Marvin Gaye and Tammi Terrell, Tamla 54149, 1967
Your Precious Love, Marvin Gaye and Tammi Terrell, Tamla 54156, 1967
If I Could Build My Whole World around You, Marvin Gaye and Tammi Terrell, Tamla 54161, 1967

By late 1966, Marvin Gaye's persona suddenly snapped into focus as Motown's most gentlemanly sex symbol, an idiosyncratic mixture of adult suaveness and adolescent awkwardness.

Mickey Stevenson and Sylvia Moy's "It Takes Two" was an endless series of memorable *mots* concerning the delights and advantages of partnership that Gaye and Weston, a soul journeyman, rendered with precise, earthy passion.

But Marvin's pairing with Tammi Terrell sparked something deeper in him. The songs had a lot to do with it, of course, especially Nick Ashford and Valerie Simpson's "Ain't No Mountain High Enough" and "Your Precious Love," which are about love as a form of spiritual transcendence. For as long as these records last, Marvin and Tammi are lovers entwined forever.

You Keep Me Hangin' On, The Supremes, Motown 1101, 1966

A tale of teenage romance as pure (if not simple) torment. This is the place where Diana inverts Aretha Franklin's "Respect." The production is a Holland-Dozier-Holland masterpiece featuring a great Morse code guitar riff, one of their patented tambourine parts, and dark, desperate bass/drum interplay. Ross, one of pop music's great self-dramatizers, never sounded more dramatic than when she half-moaned, "And there ain't nothin' I can do about it." The clincher, though, is her shiveringly pathetic "Hey, hey," at the end of the next verse.

Reach Out I'll Be There, The Four Tops, Motown 1098, 1966
Standing in the Shadows of Love, The Four Tops, Motown 1102, 1966
Bernadette, The Four Tops, Motown 1104, 1967

A grand trilogy of romantic obsession directed by Brian Holland, Lamont Dozier, and Eddie Holland in the same half-macabre mode Orson Welles brought to *Touch of Evil*, although the scale is mammoth enough for *Citizen Kane*. Levi Stubbs stars as a man who experiences lust and love as forms of identity crisis.

With the assistance of the Tops and the Funk Brothers, H-D-H worked out themes that are unmistakably adult and portrayed them with such grace that their development was finally worthy of tragedy. In their original form – as 45's – these productions were pristine (no LP or CD achieves quite the same sonic resolution).

"Bernadette" portrays a man who might today be described as a love addict. Stubbs insists that in Bernadette he's found what the entire world wishes it had and swears to devote himself to protecting his treasure. He concludes by begging her abjectly to keep on loving and needing *him*. Neither H-D-H nor anyone else ever came up with a more psychologically unsettling character sketch. Jamerson's bass line encapsulated all of this emotional turmoil with just four strings.

"Standing in the Shadows of Love" is damned near as scarifying, and it's an even better showcase for the rhythm section. The bongo breakdown at the bridge, the charging drums all the way through, create a sense of pulsation that represents with bone-chilling accuracy the lyrical portrait of a man who knows only that something has gone drastically wrong. The record is built around foreboding. "I'm tryin' not to cry out loud," Stubbs shouts, "Ya know cryin', it ain't gonna help me now." He's mystified: "What'd I do to cause you all this grief? Now, what'd I say to make you wanna leave?" The remorseless beat leaves him no way out.

With its racehorse clip-clop rhythm, agonized flute counter-melody aswirl in haunting echo, and ultimate stentorian Stubbs vocal, "Reach Out I'll Be There" ranks as one of the half-dozen greatest records anybody has ever made. It's certainly one of the biggest sounding, dwarfing the likes of Phil Spector's Wall of Sound by using what sounds like half of the Detroit Symphony as an adjunct rhythm section. Stubbs shouts like a man flung into an abyss of misery. As in "Standing in the Shadows of Love," he's awash in confusion; as in "Bernadette," passion deludes him completely. When he invites his lover to reach out for the shelter of his love, he's really proposing that she join him in his agony. The measure of this record's greatness is that anybody in his right mind would be inclined to take Stubbs up on his offer. Yet that also sets up the more abject and conscious miseries of the songs that followed, because only when a love runs this deep can it crash so profoundly. This was the glory of the Four Tops, of Holland-Dozier-Holland, and, of course, of Motown.

HONORABLE MENTION

The Way You Do the Things You Do, The Temptations, Gordy 7028, 1964
In My Lonely Room, Martha and the Vandellas, Gordy 7031, 1964
Baby I Need Your Loving, The Four Tops, Motown 1062, 1964
My Smile Is Just a Frown Turned Upside Down, Carolyn Crawford, Motown 1064, 1964
You're a Wonderful One, Marvin Gaye, Tamla 54093, 1964
Every Little Bit Hurts, Brenda Holloway, Tamla 54094, 1964
Hey Harmonica Man, Stevie Wonder, Tamla 54096, 1964
Too Many Fish in the Sea, The Marvelettes, Tamla 54105, 1964
How Sweet It Is (To Be Loved by You), Marvin Gaye, Tamla 54107, 1964
Needle in a Haystack, The Velvelettes, VIP 25007, 1964
He Was Really Sayin' Somethin', The Velvelettes, VIP 25013, 1964

The Greatest Hits/From the Beginning, The Miracles, Tamla TS2-254, 1965
Don't Look Back, The Temptations, Gordy 7047, 1965
Ask the Lonely, The Four Tops, Motown 1073, 1965
I Can't Help Myself, The Four Tops, Motown 1076, 1965
It's the Same Old Song, The Four Tops, Motown 1081, 1965
Something about You, The Four Tops, Motown 1084, 1965
My World Is Empty without You, The Supremes, Motown 1089, 1965
When I'm Gone, Brenda Holloway, Tamla 54111, 1965
I'll Be Doggone, Marvin Gaye, Tamla 54112, 1965
Ain't That Peculiar, Marvin Gaye, Tamla 54122, 1965
Don't Mess with Bill, The Marvelettes, Tamla 54126, 1965
Going to a Go Go, The Miracles, Tamla 54127, 1965
Darling Baby, The Elgins, VIP 25029, 1965
Get Ready, The Temptations, Gordy 7049, 1966
Ain't Too Proud to Beg, The Temptations, Gordy 7054, 1966
(I Know) I'm Losing You, The Temptations, Gordy 7057, 1966
Shake Me, Wake Me (When It's Over), The Four Tops, Motown 1090, 1966
Love Is Like an Itching in My Heart, The Supremes, Motown 1094, 1966
Loving You Is Sweeter than Ever, The Four Tops, Motown 1096, 1966
You Can't Hurry Love, The Supremes, Motown 1097, 1966
What Becomes of the Brokenhearted, Jimmy Ruffin, Soul 35022, 1966
I've Passed this Way Before, Jimmy Ruffin, Soul 35027, 1966
Road Runner, Junior Walker and the All Stars, Soul ss-703, 1966
This Old Heart of Mine (Is Weak for You), The Isley Brothers, Tamla 54128, 1966
One More Heartache, Marvin Gaye, Tamla 54129, 1966
I Guess I'll Always Love You, The Isley Brothers, Tamla 54135, 1966
A Place in the Sun, Stevie Wonder, Tamla 54139, 1966
The Hunter Gets Captured by the Game, The Marvelettes, Tamla 54143, 1966

Heaven Must Have Sent You, The Elgins, VIP 25037, 1966
Jimmy Ruffin Sings Top Ten, Jimmy Ruffin, Soul s-704, 1967
Jimmy Mack, Martha and the Vandellas, Gordy 7058, 1967
You're My Everything, The Temptations, Gordy 7063, 1967
I Wish It Would Rain, The Temptations, Gordy 7068, 1967
Love Is Here and Now You're Gone, The Supremes, Motown 1103, 1967
The Supremes Sing Holland-Dozier-Holland, The Supremes, Motown MS650, 1967
The Four Tops Reach Out, The Four Tops, Motown MS-660, 1967
Gonna Give Her All the Love I've Got, Jimmy Ruffin, Soul 35032, 1967
Take Me in Your Arms and Love Me, Gladys Knight and the Pips, Soul 35033, 1967
I Heard It through the Grapevine, Gladys Knight and the Pips, Soul 35039, 1967
Travelin' Man, Stevie Wonder, Tamla 54147, 1967
More Love, Smokey Robinson and the Miracles, Tamla 54152, 1967
I Second That Emotion, Smokey Robinson and the Miracles, Tamla 54159, 1967
United, Marvin Gaye and Tammi Terrell, Tamla TS-277, 1967
I Was Made to Love Her, Stevie Wonder, Tamla TS-279967, 1967

1968–1970

Love Child, Diana Ross and the Supremes, Motown 1135, 1968

This most frantic and confessional of all Supremes records represents Motown turning toward more explicit commentary. But the song presents itself in such personal terms – "No child of mine'll be bearin' / The name of shame I've been wearin'" – and the arrangement is so glossy that it's easy to miss the fact that Motown's politics, which always centered on personal advancement as the most desirable form of social progress, hadn't really changed at all. Which at least keeps the disc timeless.

I Heard It through the Grapevine, Marvin Gaye, Tamla 54176, 1968

Marvin Gaye's unique perspective on life and love didn't come through completely until "Grapevine," with its moody

evocation of innocence abused, suspicion confirmed, infidelity rampant, and peace found only through the turbulent exorcism of the beat. With stunning suddenness, Gaye found his voice.

If Holland-Dozier-Holland compiled the most agonized version of their erotic existentialism with "Reach Out I'll Be There," the only Motown record that might have matched it, grief for grief, obsession for obsession, was Gaye's masterfully sung, ornately organized exploration of what it takes to keep one human spirit whole. Gaye sang as if his life and career were at stake. Maybe they were.

Norman Whitfield created a cathedral of sound around him, from the rattlesnake bite of the opening tambourine to the chopping guitar and soaring strings. But mainly, his purpose was to support Gaye, Motown's most idiosyncratic singer, here leaping with the kind of inner pacing found in gospel music.

Gaye's "I Heard It through the Grapevine" did not effect a revolution at Motown or in pop music generally. But it powerfully foreshadowed a revolution in large part fostered by music made by Marvin Gaye.

My Whole World Ended (The Moment You Left Me), David Ruffin, Motown 1140, 1969
I Can't Get Next to You, The Temptations, Gordy 7093, 1969
Psychedelic Shack, The Temptations, Gordy 7096, 1969

The year 1969 was Motown's moment of great transition. Not only had H-D-H left but the structure of some of the company's most important acts was changing, too, whether it was Stevie Wonder's voice and style or the departure of David Ruffin from the Temptations. Ruffin had one last moment of glory with "My Whole World Ended," one in a series of titles Motown chose with bittersweet irony (the follow-up to the Four Tops' first big hit was "It's the Same Old Song"; the final number Diana Ross and the Supremes would do would be "Someday We'll Be Together").

The reign of vocal harmony, which had been the center point of soul groups since the late forties, had ended, to be replaced by a sound centered in rhythm and played out with rock band instrumentation. "I Can't Get Next to You" was a fine compromise between the two approaches, a funk beat with the harmony intact on top. But it remained for "Psychedelic Shack," released at the very end of the decade, to completely shatter the Tempts' earlier image as soul's slickest group. "Shack" picks up on all the innovations Sly Stone and James Brown had been making with their bands and reinterprets them in terms of Motown's recording studio techniques.

I Want You Back, The Jackson 5, Motown 1157, 1969

Because Michael Jackson so dearly loves categorizing his own achievements, it's tempting to invent titled accolades for his greatest one: All-Time Greatest Debut Single, Best-Ever Performance by a Preteen, Most Uncanny Representation of Adult Passion by a Prepubescent. Not to mention Record That Most Decisively Ensured Motown's Future in the Seventies. The rhythm section keeps the music distinctively in the Motown groove, but the guitar line marks the company's first really authoritative use of the funk advances pioneered by Sly and the Family Stone. Most importantly, this was the debut of That Voice.

Michael Jackson, singing an adult love song in the voice of an eleven-year-old, making you buy it both ways – it first stunned you, then shattered all of your expectations.

War, Edwin Starr, Gordy 7101, 1970

The greatest index I know of how far out of favor the war in Vietnam had fallen – since the shrewd seat-of-the-pants marketers at Motown would never have issued anything so oppositional if antiwar opinion hadn't been a foregone conclusion. Another Norman Whitfield production, it uses funk rudiments similar to those the Temptations' records were beginning to explore. But this time, the psychedelic frenzy was whipped to the edge of a mercilessly bad trip. Starr brawled it out bar after bar with fuzz guitars and tambourines. Foregone conclusion or not, this wasn't preaching to the converted; it was a full-fledged, unflinching contemplation of the horrors of dying in the mud for no good reason.

If I Were Your Woman, Gladys Knight and the Pips, Soul 35078, 1970

With the careers of so many of the company's biggest stars in flux, the late sixties proved to be an ideal moment for a variety of veteran but less distinguished

soul stars to test themselves. "If I Were Your Woman," one of the most adult love songs the label ever released, gave Knight a clearer musical identity and opened the way for the series of ballads which made her a bigger star in the seventies than anyone ever dreamed she'd be.

The End of Our Road, Marvin Gaye, Tamla 54195, 1970
Heaven Help Us All, Stevie Wonder, Tamla 54200, 1970
As an era came to an end, the Motown production line didn't break down. It grew outdated and was discarded in a variety of ways. The stories these two records tell beautifully set up the breakouts and breakthroughs to come. Marvin, of course, cast his version in the guise of a simple tale of heartbreak. Stevie, just as naturally, rendered his in the terms of a cosmic social cause. Each sang wonderfully, with delicate grace, splendid assurance, and the power of a man whose time had come.

HONORABLE MENTION

. . . Free at Last, Dr. Martin Luther King, Jr., Gordy GS-929, 1968
Walk Away Renee, The Four Tops, Motown 1119, 1968
Merry Christmas from Motown, Various artists, Motown MS-681, 1968
The End of Our Road, Gladys Knight and the Pips, Soul 35042, 1968
If You Can Want, Smokey Robinson and the Miracles, Tamla 54162, 1968
Ain't Nothing like the Real Thing, Marvin Gaye and Tammi Terrell, Tamla 54163, 1968
Take Me in Your Arms (Rock Me a Little While), The Isley Brothers, Tamla 54164, 1968
You're All I Need to Get By, Marvin Gaye and Tammi Terrell, Tamla 54169, 1968
For Once in My Life, Stevie Wonder, Tamla 54174, 1968
Twenty-Five Miles, Edwin Starr, Gordy 7083, 1969
Diana Ross Presents the Jackson 5, The Jackson 5, Motown MS-700, 1969
What Does It Take (To Win Your Love), Junior Walker and the All Stars, Soul 35062, 1969
The Nitty Gritty, Gladys Knight and the Pips, Soul 35063, 1969
Baby, I'm for Real, The Originals, Soul 35066, 1969

These Eyes, Junior Walker and the All Stars, Soul 35067, 1969
Friendship Train, Gladys Knight and the Pips, Soul 35068, 1969
The Prime of Shorty Long, Shorty Long, Soul SS-719, 1969
That's How Heartaches Are Made, The Marvelettes, Tamla 54186, 1969
Marvin Gaye and His Girls, Marvin Gaye, Tammi Terrell, Mary Wells, Kim Weston, Tamla 293, 1969
The Bells, The Originals, Soul 35069, 1970
ABC, The Jackson 5, Motown 1163, 1970
The Love You Save, The Jackson 5, Motown 1166, 1970
I'll Be There, The Jackson 5, Motown 1171, 1970
Stoned Love, The Supremes, Motown 1172, 1970
Signed, Sealed, Delivered (I'm Yours), Stevie Wonder, Tamla 54196, 1970
The Tears of a Clown, Smokey Robinson and the Miracles, Tamla 54199, 1970
Signed, Sealed & Delivered, Stevie Wonder, Tamla TS-304, 1970
It's a Shame, The Spinners, VIP 25057, 1970

1971–1975

What's Going On, Marvin Gaye, Tamla 54201, 1971
What's Going On, Marvin Gaye, Tamla TS-310, 1971

Having taken so long to find himself artistically, Marvin Gaye crafted an album that revolutionized popular music, a song cycle in the fashion of the Beatles, a funk concept LP to match any of Sly and the Family Stone's, social commentary to rival the young Bob Dylan's, sung as sweetly as the best of Otis Redding, played with as much sense of groove as classic Motown itself. The Funk Brothers were cut loose to play as freely as if they and Gaye really did comprise a band of long-standing mutual sympathy. Taken together, these eight songs ushered in a new era of adult black pop. If Motown's greatest glory was its nurturing of visionary artists making utterly personal statements in a totally commercial context, then *What's Going On* may be the company's proudest achievement. More miraculously, Gaye managed to encapsulate all of this into a single that expressed every nuance of that vision.

"What's Going On," with its almost weightless atmosphere, was as startling because of the relaxed confidence with which Marvin sang as for its multiple expansions of the soul format. And amid its denunciations of war, bigotry, and poverty, it never – ever, not for a note – lost sight of its most important purpose: To affirm that love has the power to transform the world. That's why the band's so important – you can't make music like this without surrounding yourself with loved ones.

Where I'm Coming From, Stevie Wonder, Tamla TS-308, 1971
Superstition, Stevie Wonder, Tamla 54226, 1972
Music of My Mind, Stevie Wonder, Tamla T-314L, 1972
Talking Book, Stevie Wonder, Tamla T-319L, 1972
Innervisions, Stevie Wonder, Tamla T-326L, 1973
Fulfillingness' First Finale, Stevie Wonder, Tamla T6-332S1, 1975

Stevie Wonder's early forays into self-production did not immediately result in confirmation of his visionary artistry. *Where I'm Coming From* was tentative. But Wonder's best album, *Music of My Mind*, kicked off by the single "Superstition" (originally written as an instrumental for British rock guitarist Jeff Beck), focused Stevie's new sound. He proceeded to rattle off a series of remarkable albums in a streak that lasted the rest of the decade. *Music of My Mind*, *Talking Book*, and *Innervisions* gave a sense of a new Stevie Wonder, as much an adult as Marvin Gaye but with a view of the world which turned outward far more than inward.

In "Living for the City," from *Innervisions*, Stevie created a sound montage the equal of anything the Beatles or Frank Zappa had dreamed up and did it with such a memorable melody, with such groove and verve, that it became a hit single. If *Fulfillingness' First Finale* wasn't quite up to the standard of its three predecessors, it fell short of a mark only Stevie himself could match.

Smiling Faces Sometimes, The Undisputed Truth, Gordy 7108, 1971
Papa Was a Rollin' Stone, The Temptations, Gordy 7121, 1972

Among the slightly paranoid pop-funk hits of the early seventies – the O'Jays'

"Back Stabbers," Curtis Mayfield's "Freddie's Dead," Marvin Gaye's "What's Going On" – "Smiling Faces" comes very near the top. The very top, however, is occupied by the Temptations' "Papa Was a Rollin' Stone." Besides being the greatest showcase the Temptations' bass voice Melvin Franklin ever had, and besides being an evocative, if ambiguous, exploration of the issue of male roles in black nuclear family life, "Papa Was a Rollin' Stone" was Norman Whitfield's ultimate production showcase, especially its extended opening – a melange of strings, synthesizer, wah-wah guitar, and orchestral (as opposed to mouth) harp – and the rhythm bed, which brings the jazz-funk of Miles Davis's *Bitches Brew* back on home.

Never Can Say Goodbye, The Jackson 5, Motown 1179, 1971
Got to Be There, Michael Jackson, Motown 1191, 1971

In which the greatest teenage singer of all time finally finds out what he's really good at – ballads. The J5 hit flirts with being a rhythm number but Michael's initial solo hit is unflinchingly mushy – and marvelous – from top to bottom.

Way Back Home, Junior Walker and the All Stars, Soul 35090, 1971

Whenever Motown seemed about to descend into complete city-slickness, somebody or something always dragged it back to the roots. In 1971 it was Junior Walker's raspy blues and melancholic vocal on a song that opened with a declaration designed to shock the uninitiated –"There's good and bad things about the South, boy / And some leave a bitter taste in my mouth. . . . But we won't talk about that 'cause it's understood / Everybody sees the bad but what about the good?" From there on, every single detail offers up a flavor of unbelievable, half-forbidden sweetness. Nor is the subject simple nostalgia – instead, it's the complex nostalgia of a people driven out of their homes by racism and economics and transferred to a world in every way colder. Walker isn't mourning his youth; he's mourning the South that nurtured the culture that bore its fullest flower in the North. Though he knew the exact dangers of over-sentimentalizing the facts, he still wouldn't stop, not because he was a modern, "ironic" man but because (to quote Sly Stone) "blood's thicker than the

mud," and a man can't help but love what he loves, no matter how hateful it may be.
If you still don't get it, try using "Way Back Home" as a soundtrack while rereading James Baldwin's *The Fire Next Time*.

People . . . Hold On, Eddie Kendricks, Tamla T-315L, 1972
Keep On Truckin', parts 1 and 2, Eddie Kendricks, Tamla 54238, 1973

For Eddie Kendricks the arrival of disco served as a sort of liberation. Always overshadowed by David Ruffin in the Temptations, his high, thin tenor was better suited to the more brittle tonality of the new dance records. Though this album further extended the new Motown dance groove, it was "Keep On Truckin'," a Number One hit at both pop and R&B stations, that really drove the point home.

Let's Get It On, Marvin Gaye, Tamla T-329-1, 1973
A Quiet Storm, Smokey Robinson, Tamla T6-337S1, 1975

With dancing and rhythm claiming mass attention, what was left for the great Motown sensualists, its fine ballad singers and masters of the make-out groove?
The two best-made records that were among the best of their careers, records that did not ignore the advances in rhythm and technology but that remained consistent with the artists' earlier material. *Let's Get It On*, Marvin's great follow-up to *What's Going On*, sounded like it was replying to all the most intimate questions he'd asked himself while making his great musical and sociological study of American culture. This isn't a record about romance or heartbreak or finding a partner, though it encompasses all of those things. More than any other great album, *Let's Get It On* is about sex. And in its sinuous hedonism, Marvin Gaye found his place among the great music makers of that dance-dominated era.
Smokey Robinson's transition to solo stardom was more delicate and difficult; he seemed unsure. The tense, dense *Quiet Storm* didn't pull him all the way to his classic singing and songwriting, but it did give him a format: a new brand of dreamy, smooth make-out

music. It had sufficient impact that within a few years, a whole new "Quiet Storm" radio format came into being.

HONORABLE MENTION

Just My Imagination (Running Away with Me), The Temptations, Gordy 7105, 1971
We Can Work It Out, Stevie Wonder, Tamla 54202, 1971
Mercy Mercy Me (The Ecology), Marvin Gaye, Tamla 54207, 1971
If You Really Love Me, Stevie Wonder, Tamla 54208, 1971
Inner City Blues (Make Me Wanna Holler), Marvin Gaye, Tamla 54209, 1971
If I Were Your Woman, Gladys Knight and the Pips, Soul ss-731, 1971
Exposed, Valerie Simpson, Tamla TS-311, 1971
One Dozen Roses, Smokey Robinson and the Miracles, Tamla T-312L, 1971
Heart of the Matter, King Floyd, VIP VIPS-407, 1971
Neither One of Us (Wants to Be the First to Say Goodbye), Gladys Knight and the Pips, Soul 35098, 1972
Rockin' Robin, Michael Jackson, Motown 1197, 1972
I Wanna Be Where You Are, Michael Jackson, Motown 1202, 1972
Ben, Michael Jackson, Motown 1207, 1972
Trouble Man, Marvin Gaye, Tamla T-322L, 1972
The Mack (soundtrack), Willie Hutch, Motown M-766L, 1973
Daddy Could Swear (I Declare), Gladys Knight and the Pips, Soul 35105, 1973
Girl You Need a Change of Mind, parts 1 and 2, Eddie Kendricks, Tamla 54230, 1973
You Are the Sunshine of My Life, Stevie Wonder, Tamla 54232, 1973
Let's Get It On, Marvin Gaye, Tamla 54234, 1973
Higher Ground, Stevie Wonder, Tamla 54235, 1973
Come Get to This/Distant Lover, Marvin Gaye, Tamla 54241, 1973
Living for the City, Stevie Wonder, Tamla 54242, 1973
My Mistake (Was to Love You), Diana Ross and Marvin Gaye, Motown 1269, 1974
Machine Gun, The Commodores, Motown 1307, 1974
Machine Gun, The Commodores, Motown M6-79881, 1974
Shoe Shine, The Dynamic Superiors, Motown 1324, 1974

Dancing Machine, The Jackson 5, Motown M6-780S1, 1974
You Haven't Done Nothin', Stevie Wonder, Tamla 54252, 1974
Distant Lover (live version), Marvin Gaye, Tamla 54253, 1974

1976–1980

Songs in the Key of Life, Stevie Wonder, Tamla T13-340C2, 1976

Stevie's most expansive song cycle – two full albums and an LP – didn't necessarily represent a tremendous musical advance, and his lyrics had grown so involuted that they often pushed the limits of intelligibility. But *Songs in the Key of Life*, with its multiple Grammy awards and string of unconventionally structured hit singles, established once and for all that Stevie Wonder was the greatest compositional and recording genius of the soul/rock generation.

Easy, The Commodores, Motown 1418, 1977
Three Times a Lady, The Commodores, Motown 1443, 1978

The Commodores reached an ever-widening public with a series of syrupy but stirring love ballads, composed and sung by saxophonist Lionel Richie. "Easy" added a zipping guitar solo; "Three Times a Lady" kept the schmaltz pure and sweet and went all the way to Number One. With such songs, during the anomalous Urban Cowboy trend, the Commodores became the first Motown act to breach Nashville's barriers.

Here, My Dear, Marvin Gaye, Tamla T-364LP2, 1978
Stevie Wonder's Journey through the Secret Life of Plants, Stevie Wonder, Tamla T13-371N2, 1979

Motown's main eccentrics as far out on the limb as they are – or anybody else – ever got. Marvin made *Here, My Dear* in order to have royalty income to give to his ex-wife. Obsessive, offhanded, snarling, sardonic, and silly, the music holds up surprisingly well for a project that seemed determined to prove the adage, "When you seek revenge, first dig two graves."

RECORDED LIVE
LITTLE STEVIE WONDER THE 12 YEAR OLD GENIUS

INCLUDED IN THIS ALBUM *FINGER TIPS* PART 1&2

Meantime, the world's most famous blind soul composer enlisted himself to write a soundtrack for a film about the sensitivities of the vegetable kingdom. The audacity of the score, which has the compositional unity of a sonata and lyrics written from the plants' point of view, ought to have made it an object of fascination for Wonder cultists. Instead, its beauties were ignored in favor of cheap laughs at its supposed simpleminded mysticism. It remains, for those with ears to hear it, the last genuinely ambitious album of Wonder's career.

I'm a Sucker for Your Love, Teena Marie, Gordy 7169, 1979
Bustin' out of L Seven, Rick James, Gordy G7-984R1, 1979

Rick James was the closest thing to a white rock star Motown ever produced. He specialized in the kind of elaborate vulgarity best known among heavy metal acts, although, to be fair, his punk funk was far hipper than any metal (or all but the most rarified punk), and the best of it brought together rock power and funk-groove depth in a singularly fascinating way. *Bustin' out of L Seven* stands as his best album, just before his commercial peak, equally devoted to the hedonistic delights of herbs and honeys.
James not only had an eye for girls, he had an ear for them. His first discovery was Teena Marie, a chunky white punk funkster whose dalliance with black, male grooves and unabashed sexuality (the title wasn't just suggestive)

anticipated that later Motor City wunderkind, Madonna.

Cruisin', Smokey Robinson, Tamla 54306, 1979

With "Cruisin'" Smokey reassumed his mantle as the smooch music master. Not quite a car song, flirting with all sorts of ambiguous sexual postures, extended but totally centered, "Cruisin'" moves with the weighty elegance of a vintage Cadillac. It gave Smokey his best hit since leaving the Miracles.

Master Blaster (Jammin'), Stevie Wonder, Tamla 54317, 1980

Stevie Wonder's tribute to reggae superhero Bob Marley. Motown's only full-scale dalliance with the Caribbean beat during the dance decade (though Lionel Richie dipped his toe in those waters a bit more on his second solo album) was Stevie's strongest recovery from the debacle of *Secret Life of Plants*.

HONORABLE MENTION

Don't Leave Me This Way, Thelma Houston, Tamla 54278, 1976
Smokey's Family Robinson, Smokey Robinson, Tamla T6-341S1, 1976
Brick House, The Commodores, Motown 1425, 1977
Sir Duke, Stevie Wonder, Tamla 54281, 1977
Mary Jane, Rick James, Gordy 7162, 1978

Bustin' Out, Rick James, Gordy 7167, 1979
Heaven Must Have Sent You, Bonnie Pointer, Motown 1459, 1979
Sail On, The Commodores, Motown 1466, 1979
Behind the Groove, Teena Marie, Gordy 7184, 1980
Let's Get Serious, Jermaine Jackson, Motown 1469, 1980
Upside Down, Diana Ross, Motown 1494, 1980
Warm Thoughts, Smokey Robinson, Tamla T8367M1, 1980
Hotter than July, Stevie Wonder, Tamla T8-373M1, 1980

1980s

Happy Birthday, Stevie Wonder, Motown 4517MGA, 1981
The Crown, Gary Byrd and the G. B. Experience, Wondirection 4507, 1983

Stevie Wonder remained the most political member of the Motown family, and although his eighties records often seemed internally adrift (or, like "I Just Called to Say I Love You," cynically cranked out), "Happy Birthday," his tribute to Dr. Martin Luther King, recalls the joyous bursts of energy which typified his late sixties releases. And "Happy Birthday" has the rare distinction of being a political pop record that got results; Wonder spearheaded the drive for the King birthday holiday, for which his song became the anthem.
Gary Byrd, the only artist to release anything on Wonder's Wondirection label, is a well-known black radio personality in New York. His early, relatively subdued rap single offers kids a lesson in black history and pride with a specifically antiracist tag.

Lionel Richie, Lionel Richie, Motown 6007ML, 1982

At his worst Lionel Richie without the Commodores has seemed like nothing so much as the black Kenny Rogers, making noises as big and pretty as they are false and hollow. But at his best, he was one of R&B's finest eighties balladeers, and on his first solo album, he was more often than not working near the peak of his ability. Indeed, since hit corn like "Truly," "My Love," and "You Are" is mostly mood music anyhow, you're better off dealing with it a side at a time as the background soul it's meant to be.

Somebody's Watching Me, Rockwell, Motown 1702MF, 1983

Rockwell's real name is Kennedy Gordy, and as a son of Motown's founder, he may very well feel over-observed. Actually, his one hit is a witty, pointed pop-funk satire of paranoia. At least I think so. Don't you? Huh?

Dial My Heart, The Boys, Motown MOT 53301, 1988

The Boys' effervescent "Dial My Heart," which balances hip-hop and teenybop harmony, charms you into believing in all sorts of futures: the group's, Motown's, maybe even – given the links – your own. At the very least, it's still the Sound of Young America. And by the way, did I tell you about the new Smokey album? I hear Stevie's working on something. . . . Did you catch the Four Tops at the Rock & Roll Hall of Fame?

HONORABLE MENTION

You and I, Switch, Gordy 7199, 1981
What's Your Name, The DeBarges, Gordy 7203, 1981
Super Freak (parts 1 and 2), Rick James, Gordy 7205, 1981
It Must Be Magic, Teena Marie, Gordy 1004M1, 1981
Street Songs, Rick James, Gordy G8-1002M1, 1981
Lady (You Bring Me Up), The Commodores, Motown 1514, 1981
Right in the Middle (Of Falling in Love), Betty Lavette, Motown 1532, 1982
Let It Whip, Dazz Band, Motown 4505MG, 1982
Tell Me a Lie, Betty Lavette, Motown 6000ML, 1982
Dance wit' Me, parts 1 and 2, Rick James, Gordy 1619GF, 1982
Ebony Eyes, Rick James and Smokey Robinson, Gordy 1714GF, 1983
The Mary Jane Girls, The Mary Jane Girls, Gordy 6040GL, 1983
Nightshift, The Commodores, Motown 1773MF, 1984
Rhythm of the Night, DeBarge, Gordy 1770GF, 1985
Who's Holding Donna Now, DeBarge, Gordy 1793GF, 1985
Part-Time Lover, Stevie Wonder, Tamla 18085F, 1985
El DeBarge, El DeBarge, Gordy 6181GL, 1986

Lyrics from the following songs have been used with the permission of Jobete Music Co., Inc., and Stone Diamond Music Corporation.

Money (That's What I Want)
Berry Gordy/
Janie Bradford
© November 1959, Jobete Music Co., Inc./Stone Agate Music

Dancing in the Street
Ivy J. Hunter/William Stevenson/Marvin Gaye
© July 1964, Jobete Music Co., Inc./Stone Agate Music

Shop Around
William Robinson/
Berry Gordy
© April 1960, Jobete Music Co., Inc.

The Tracks of My Tears
William Robinson/
Marvin Tarplin/Warren Moore
© June 1965, Jobete Music Co., Inc.

Pride and Joy
Norman Whitfield/
William Stevenson/
Marvin Gaye
© February 1963, Jobete Music Co., Inc./Stone Agate Music

I Heard It through the Grapevine
Norman Whitfield/
Barrett Strong
© August 1966, Stone Agate Music

Ain't No Mountain High Enough
Nickolas Ashford/Valerie Simpson
© February 1967, Jobete Music Co., Inc.

My Guy
William Robinson
© May 1964, Jobete Music Co., Inc.

Do You Love Me
Berry Gordy
© June 1962, Jobete Music Co., Inc.

Fingertips
Clarence Paul/Henry Cosby
© November 1962, Jobete Music Co., Inc./Stone Agate Music

Please Mr. Postman
William Garrett/Georgia Dobbins/Brian Holland/Freddie Gorman/Robert Bateman
© August 1961, Jobete Music Co., Inc./Stone Agate Music

Nowhere to Run
Brian Holland/Lamont Dozier/Eddie Holland
© January 1965, Stone Agate Music

Function at the Junction
Fredrick Long/Eddie Holland
© March 1966, Stone Agate Music

What Becomes of the Brokenhearted
James Dean/Paul Riser/William Weatherspoon
© March 1966, Stone Agate Music

Shotgun
Autry DeWalt
© January 1965, Stone Agate Music

If I Were Your Woman
Clay McMurray/Pamela Sawyer/Gloria Jones
© October 1970, Jobete Music Co., Inc.

I Can't Help Myself (Sugar Pie, Honey Bunch)
Brian Holland/Lamont Dozier/Eddie Holland
© April 1965, Stone Agate Music

Baby I Need Your Loving
Brian Holland/Lamont Dozier/Eddie Holland
© July 1964, Stone Agate Music

Reach Out I'll Be There
Brian Holland/Lamont Dozier/Eddie Holland
© August 1966, Stone Agate Music

Love Is Here and Now You're Gone
Brian Holland/Lamont Dozier/Eddie Holland
© October 1966, Stone Agate Music

Stop! In the Name of Love
Brian Holland/Lamont Dozier/Eddie Holland
© January 1965, Stone Agate Music

Shake Me, Wake Me (When It's Over)
Brian Holland/Lamont Dozier/Eddie Holland
© January 1966, Stone Agate Music

Get Ready
William Robinson
© January 1966, Jobete Music Co., Inc.

My Girl
William Robinson/
Ronald White
© December 1964, Jobete Music Co., Inc.

The Way You Do the Things You Do
William Robinson/
Robert Rogers
© March 1964, Jobete Music Co., Inc.

Someday We'll Be Together
Harvey Fuqua/John Bristol/Jackey Beavers
© October 1961, Jobete Music Co., Inc./Stone Agate Music

You Can't Hurry Love
Brian Holland/Lamont Dozier/Eddie Holland
© June 1965, Stone Agate Music

Where Did Our Love Go
Brian Holland/Lamont Dozier/Eddie Holland
© May 1964, Stone Agate Music

You Keep Me Hanging On
Brian Holland/Lamont Dozier/Eddie Holland
© August 1966, Stone Agate Music

ABC
The Corporation
© February 1970, Jobete Music Co., Inc.

Never Can Say Goodbye
Clifton Davis
© December 1970, Jobete Music Co., Inc./Portable Music Co.

Three Times a Lady
Lionel Richie
© May 1978, Jobete Music Co., Inc./Libren Music

War
Norman Whitfield/
Barrett Strong
© February 1970, Stone Agate Music

What's Going On
Marvin Gaye/Renaldo Benson/Alfred Cleveland
© December 1970, Jobete Music Co., Inc./Stone Agate Music

Mercy Mercy Me (The Ecology)
Marvin Gaye
© July 1971, Jobete Music Co., Inc.

Let's Get It On
Marvin Gaye/Ed Townsend
© February 1973, Jobete Music Co., Inc./Stone Diamond Music Corporation

You Are the Sunshine of My Life
Stevie Wonder
© October 1972, Jobete Music Co., Inc./Black Bull Music

A Place in the Sun
Ron Miller/Bryan Wells
© August 1966, Jobete Music Co., Inc./Stone Diamond Music Corporation

Super Freak
Rick James/Alonzo Miller
© June 1981, Jobete Music Co., Inc./Stone City Music/Stone Diamond Music Corporation

Portions of the following songs appear in the text and discography:

Yester-Me, Yester-You, Yesterday by Ron Miller and Bryan Wells, © 1966 Jobete Music Co., Inc.; **Come See about Me** by Eddie Holland, Lamont Dozier, and Brian Holland, © 1964 Stone Agate Music; **The Love I Saw in You Was Just a Mirage** by William Robinson and Marvin Tarplin, © 1967 Jobete Music Co., Inc.; **You're a Wonderful One** by Eddie Holland, Lamont Dozier, and Brian Holland, © 1964 Stone Agate Music; **Heat Wave** by Brian Holland, Lamont Dozier, and Eddie Holland, © 1965, 1966 Jobete Music Co., Inc.; **Back in My Arms Again** by Eddie Holland, Lamont Dozier, and Brian Holland, © 1965 Stone Agate Music Division; **The Tracks of My Tears** by William Robinson, © 1965, 1967 Jobete Music Co., Inc.; **Standing in the Shadows of Love** by Eddie Holland, Lamont Dozier, and Brian Holland, © 1966, 1967, 1968 Jobete Music Co., Inc.; **Love Child** by Pam Sawyer, R. Dean Taylor, Frank Wilson, and Deke Richards, © 1968 Jobete Music Co., Inc.; **Way Back Home** by Johnny Bristol, Gladys Knight, and Wilton Felder, © 1973 Four Knights Music.

The
MOTOWN
ALBUM

PHOTO CREDITS
—
AUTHORS'
BIOGRAPHIES

Ben Fong-Torres, columnist and feature writer at the *San Francisco Chronicle*, is a former senior editor of *Rolling Stone* magazine, where his interview subjects included Marvin Gaye, Stevie Wonder, Paul McCartney, Diana Ross, the Rolling Stones, Bob Dylan, the Jackson 5, Gladys Knight and the Pips, Ray Charles, Smokey Robinson and the Miracles, and the Temptations. He edited *The Rolling Stone Interviews, Volume Two* and contributes articles to a variety of publications. Currently, he is working on a biography of Gram Parsons.

Dave Marsh is the author of the best-selling Bruce Springsteen biographies, *Born to Run* and *Glory Days*, and eleven other books about popular music, including *The Heart of Rock and Soul: The 1001 Greatest Singles Ever Made*. He edited the first two editions of *The Rolling Stone Record Guide* and is currently editing the unpublished papers of folksinger Woody Guthrie. A founder of *Creem* and former associate editor of *Rolling Stone*, Marsh edits "Rock & Roll Confidential," a newsletter about rock and politics, and frequently contributes to *Village Voice* and *Playboy*.

Elvis Mitchell is a freelance writer and frequent contributor to *Rolling Stone*, *Village Voice*, and *California* magazine, where he is a contributing editor. His film reviews are broadcast on National Public Radio.

UPTO U

THE MIRACLES · MARY
MARVELETTES
THE CONTOURS MARTHA & V
MARVIN GAYE   THE SU
BILL MURRAY   CHOKER CAMPB